JJ GREEN

JJ Green is an actor, writer and disability-in-the-arts consultant. His career thus far includes acting at the National Theatre, London, Universal Studios, Florida, and Walt Disney theme parks. As a writer he led on the project *An Adapter Plug Guide to Autism in the Arts*, which launched through Equity UK in 2021. *A-Typical Rainbow*, his first professional play, is written from an autistic and queer standpoint and created by the community it is about. He believes it is vital that autistic stories are heard, created and told by autistic people.

As a disability-in-the-arts consultant, JJ is passionate about storytelling being done accessibly, and believes that access needs being met, stories being told and opportunities being given are a vital component to making theatre the varied and inclusive art form it claims to be.

Other Titles in this Series

JJ Green

A-TYPICAL
RAINBOW

NICK HERN BOOKS

London

www.nickhernbooks.co.uk

A Nick Hern Book

A-Typical Rainbow first published in Great Britain as a paperback original in 2022 by Nick Hern Books Limited, The Glasshouse, 49a Goldhawk Road, London W12 8QP

A-Typical Rainbow copyright © 2022 JJ Green

JJ Green has asserted his right to be identified as the author of this work

Cover image: Steph Pyne

Designed and typeset by Nick Hern Books, London
Printed in Great Britain by Mimeo Ltd, Huntingdon, Cambridgeshire PE29 6XX

A CIP catalogue record for this book is available from the British Library

ISBN 978 1 83904 103 7

Woodland
CARBON
www.woodlandcarbon.co.uk
NICK HERN BOOKS
Printed on Carbon Captured paper

For my mother and all that she stood for
For Sophie and all that they are yet to stand for

&

For Jamie, who stands with me

Author's Note

This play should feel otherworldly. The lens of autism is often portrayed as an outside-looking-in matter where the world is as it is seen by neurotypical people and the oddity is the autistic character within that world. With this play I want to reverse that imagery – here I want the lines between imagination and reality to appear blurred and neurotypical standards questioned. Due to large portions of the play taking place in imagination sequences, the shift between what is real and what is not should be unclear. This is a play through the eyes of an autistic person, consequently the rest of the world needs to appear through that lens, also. A polished, precise, bright but unnerving world. Inspiration of aesthetics drawn from Wes Anderson, Lemony Snicket, Tim Burton and Dr. Seuss. The pallet is pastel and of the sixties, everything clean, neat and perfect in look. Costuming, set and lighting should also resemble this world that is so crisp, clean, colourful and polished it's beautiful but terrifying. The white picket fence and American dream presented as otherness.

Though this is not a musical, all monologues are to have themes played beneath them that swell in emotion similarly to that of musical theatre but remain spoken.

JJ Green

A-Typical Rainbow was first performed at the Turbine Theatre, London, on 30 June 2022. The cast and creative team was as follows:

BOY	JJ Green
MOTHER	Caroline Deverill
FATHER/DOCTOR	James Westphal
JAKE/DANIEL	Conor Joseph
ABBY/THOMAS/ LARA	Joy Tan
EMILY/MRS WHITEMAN/ RACHEL	Maya Manuel

Director	Bronagh Lagan
Set and Costume Designer	Frankie Gerrard
Choreographer	William Spencer
Composer and Sound Designer	Max Alexander-Taylor
Lighting Designer	Bethany Gupwell
Associate Sound Designer	Chris Czornyj
Video Designer	Matt Powell
Casting Director	Jane Deitch
Production Manager	Jack Boisseux
Deputy Stage Manager	Ryan Webster
Assistant Stage Manager	Alice Wood
Costume Supervisor	Emmy Tobitt
Stage One Bridge The Gap Placement	Sarah Jordan Verghese

For Aria Entertainment

Company Director and Producer	Katy Lipson
General Manager and Assistant Producer	Chris Matanlé
Production Coordinator	Ollie Hancock
Literary Manager and Assistant Producer	Tom Ramsay

Characters

BOY, *male presenting, has ASD. Playing age twenty to twenty-five. Slim build. Striking but non-conventionally attractive features. Intelligent, sarcastic, quick, quippy and curious, occasionally comical without knowing it.*

MOTHER/RACHEL/ENSEMBLE, *British female. Playing age thirty-five to forty. Kind, comforting, caring and compassionate yet brave and firm. She focuses on all but herself. She uses love for others to cope. A kind, slim face and build with resemblance to that of her son. Rachel is of the same age and look but far more outgoing.*

FATHER/DOCTOR/ARMY COACH/ENSEMBLE, *male. Playing age twenty-five to thirty-five. Muscular/masculine build and demeanour. 5'9"– 6ft. Must be able to convey age differences in his acting due to the fact his characters span two decades. The Father, Doctor and Army Coach are aggressive, assertive and direct. They lack any emotion that isn't anger or disdain.*

THOMAS/ABBY/LARA/WITNESS ONE, *female. Playing age twenty to thirty. An innocent and youthful but expressive face. 4'5" – 5'6". The brother, the first small love-interest, the friend. Thomas is meek, loyal, understanding but overshadowed. Abby appears fake and self-obsessed but is secretly kind, lost and struggling to find her avenue to shine. Lara is confident, strong, self-assured and motherly, aware of all those around her. These three characters are a direct development of each other, resembling the journey of youth to adulthood.*

MRS WHITEMAN/EMILY/WITNESS TWO/ENSEMBLE, *British female. No specific playing age or height so long as the actor can convey youth and adulthood well. Mrs Whiteman is stern yet unsure of herself, a professional. Emily is sharp and shallow. She is the girl we all knew in high school; entirely detestable.*

JAKE/DANIEL/EMILE/JUDGE/ENSEMBLE, *male. Playing age twenty to thirty. 5'9"– 6'2". Any look. Jake is a typical high-school bully. Daniel is kind, compassionate, fun-loving and free. For the Judge see Father/Doctor.*

Please cast as diversely as possible, where possible.

This text went to press before the end of rehearsals and so may differ slightly from the play as performed.

ACT ONE

Scene One

*A stage resembling a small house in framework only. On the
back wall are medical drawers and filing cabinets capable of
being pulled out. The house has a small bed with a rainbow
bedside lamp. A singular man (BOY) sits on a Victorian trunk
centre stage. The house is dimly lit, and the bedside lamp is on.
The stage will transform by use of puppetry and accessible
projection as the* BOY'*s monologue progresses.* MOTHER
enters. She tidies the drawers at the back of the stage.

MOTHER. Teeth brushed?

> BOY *nods.*

School bag packed?

> BOY *nods.*

Into bed then.

> BOY *jumps into bed.* MOTHER *approaches to tuck him in.*

Story of choice?

> BOY *looks to her. Beat.*

(*Tenderly.*) Fine. But quickly.

> BOY *nods.*

And only one verse.

> BOY *nods.*

*She strokes his hair and sings the opening verse of 'Over the
Rainbow'. No instrumental. Imperfect vocally.* BOY *settles
in bed. The lamp dims.* MOTHER *kisses his head and exits.*

The sound of a plane landing, seatbelt signs on. BOY *sits
upright in bed.*

BOY. Hi. I'm seven. Not literally. I am figuratively seven for the context of what we're doing now. Which is here which is this which is talking. I'm literally seven in the same way that after doing your tax return you are not literally dying. You, your bank account, happiness and parents' pride are *figurati*vely dying. Not literally dying. You may be literally dying in a month however when a Tesco meal deal starts to feel a little bit like caviar.

Me trying to explain the emotions I have is like taking a fourteen-day rambling holiday with your high-school geography teacher across the Himalayas equipped only with a pair of Crocs, a Lucozade Sport and a stick you think makes you look like Gandalf. I reach base camp when I realise I had the map upside down and I'm meant to be somewhere on the Yorkshire Dales. My brain to me is mundane. But to everyone else – it's a little broken.

I remember a child at school once bragged to me how on her last holiday she swam with dolphins. Her name was Emily and she was repellent. She was the kind of child who cartwheeled everywhere she went. She grew up into one of those people who when faced with a coffee cake stupidly staggers over to it before saying '*Well, I shouldn't but I will*', is drawn like a moth to a flame at the sight of a Gymshark logo and thinks *Love Island* is a modern-day Jane Austen novel.

Emily made fun of me because I told her what it was like to swim with mermaids in return for her swanky tale about the dolphin zoo in Florida. She told me I was mental. I wasn't mental. I have swum with mermaids. I didn't know nobody else had. I still kind of don't.

Projection shift, BOY *climbs the set and interacts with the world it becomes. Mermaid theme plays.*

A crystal-clear lavender lagoon under the shimmering light of a full moon and a million stars dotted across the dreamscape of my imagination. Sapphire tails flicked as I pulled myself out of the water, its reflection playing off my skin like the finest music so soft to sound and so vibrant to touch. I perched on the edge of a sea-moss-covered rock and picked at limpets chatting casually to my mythic company about the politics and orchestra of the ocean. A friend to sirens, salt crystalising in my hair like diamonds, watching them endlessly. I admired them dancing their aquatic waltz from crimson sunset to the birth of day behind the rainforest peaks of the nearby mountainside. I've ridden dragons behind my eyelids, bounced from Saturn to Venus on the great starry trampoline of the galaxy, fallen through time and ran with wolves in highland forest mists that exist no place but my imagination. But it's real. It's more than real, because it's better than real. I can go there. Nobody else can. It's mine. Feel the dirt under my feet, hear the conversational whispers of trees and smell the damp pine in the mist. I've fought in great battles and trapezed through the circus in the skies of my mind balancing on cloud tips and cuddling into the warmth of a thousand stars. I can change colours of objects by looking at them, hear the symphonies of household simplicities, taste the emotions in a room like sweet or bitter wine and feel life's every heartbeat breaking through my ribcage in glorious technicolour. Just don't ask me to make eye contact. (*Beat*.) I hope your dolphins were fun, Emily. Watch *Blackfish*. I kind of know how they feel. Also, I'm not mental. Syncing your thirty Pandora charms up with your menstrual cycle is mental.

Scene Two

Therapist's Office/Airplane

A woman, MOTHER, *and a man,* DOCTOR, *are sat upon the trunks, now arranged like the furniture of a doctor's office.* BOY *sits on the floor between them. The bed serves as a table.*

MOTHER. He's incredibly advanced for a seven-year-old in so many ways, but in others he. He lacks.

DOCTOR. Lacks.

MOTHER. Considerably.

DOCTOR (*to* BOY). So, tell me what these are you've drawn?

BOY. Well, that's the subconscious manifestation of all the hopes and dreams I hope to achieve in my life blended in colours that resemble eternal youth.

DOCTOR. I see, and this one?

BOY. That's London city centre in the 1830s at the dawn of the Industrial Revolution.

DOCTOR. And finally this one?

BOY. That's a zebra. Neigh. (*He makes audible clip-clop noises. Spots audience laughter. Immediately stops.*)

DOCTOR. Well, he's very good, does he have a name?

BOY. No, he's a drawing.

DOCTOR (*to* MOTHER). Have you ever considered that he maybe has Asperger's syndrome? I don't know how much you're aware of this disorder but judging from what we've seen over the last couple of weeks I would say there's a strong chance that –

BOY. Okay now is a really good time to talk about the word 'maybe'… 'Maybe' doesn't make sense. Something either is or it isn't. It's black or it's white. You either know or you don't. Let me show you just how ridiculous your word 'maybe' is.

The cast are joined by the remaining ensemble, each with their own trunks positioned on the stage to create an airplane setting. Sound effects/lighting assist in creating the illusion of being mid-flight. MOTHER *speaks in a comical peppy American accent.*

MOTHER/HOSTESS. Hi. Welcome on board this 1401 Jumbo Jet service to blatant insanity. We'll maybe be cruising at an altitude of thirty-six-thousand feet. We *may* land in water at some point during our flight if a bird *maybe* chaotically wedges itself with all the force its tiny wings can manage into one of our jet engines so please pay close attention. Your life vest *may* be located in the underpart of your seat. The doors on the cabin side may open and you *might* be able to slide down into the freezing cold shark-infested waters below. Sir, sit down.

BOY (*aside*). I've always loved *Jaws*.

MOTHER/HOSTESS. Once there, the jacket is equipped with a tiny weeny little light you can use to attract the sharks' attention or maybe mine, if I haven't been devoured, to assist you in some way unspecified. How on earth anyone thinks me in my six-inch heels, full face of make-up and exceptionally long limbs is saving you from a shark is anyone's guess. If the cabin loses pressure, *and it might*, an oxygen mask *may* drop down from the panel above your head. Please see to your own mask first or your child *may* turn blue and collapse into their *maybe* microwaved dinner.

Spoiler. It really is microwaved.

BOY. 'Maybe' makes no sense. 'Maybe' is unnerving. It implies lack of certainty. Grey area is a playground I've never been to.

Trunks are rearranged, clothing put back in trunk. The doctor's-office scene resumes.

MOTHER. Asperger's syndrome?

BOY (*comically*). Yeah from what we just saw I'd fucking say so.

DOCTOR. Yes, nothing to worry about just expect low social development, panic attacks, the occasional outburst, confused concepts in all manner of life, exceptionally poor emotional reception and very homed interests. Think of it like a cocktail of imagination with a socially awkward spritzer that occasionally screams as you try to drink it.

BOY. We've all been there.

DOCTOR. It's probably best he's taught how to integrate into society normally.

The following quote is projected onto the back wall as the DOCTOR *says it.*

'You see you start pretty much from scratch when you work with an autistic child. You have a person in the physical sense – they have hair, a nose, a mouth – but they are not people in the psychological sense. One way to look at the job of helping autistic kids is to see it as a matter of constructing a person. You have the raw materials, but you have to build the person.'

This approach is the most popular therapy for autistic children in 2022.

MOTHER. It's 1999.

DOCTOR. We'll continue to monitor him weekly. Do your best to discourage any abnormal behaviour. It's fantastic we've caught this early, it's far easier when they're young. We'll see you same time next week.

Beat.

BOY. Can we get a McDonald's on the way home.

MOTHER (*unfocused*). Of course we can, darling.

She kisses his head.

Scene Three

Parents' Bedroom

The trunks are now arranged in a way to resemble a bed.
MOTHER *and* FATHER *walk around their room preparing for bed.* BOY *sits on the edge of the stage, a Little Mermaid doll is placed in front of him. He stares at it – vacant.*

FATHER. He's just a kid with a vivid imagination, you coddle him too much.

MOTHER. Well, I think that's sort of the idea yes… He gets terribly bullied. I just think we ought to put some stock into it, that's all. He needs the support of both of us.

His reaction shows she's overstepped the mark.

I'm just saying that he needs time and attention. He just needs to be given the best chances in life – that's all. A little adjusting, tweaking. He's got worlds in him –

FATHER. I'll continue to pay for it if that's what you're asking.

MOTHER. You know that's not what I'm asking.

FATHER. Isn't it?

MOTHER. You know it's not.

Long beat.

Are you going to tell me what's bothering you more than this is? Something clearly is.

FATHER. You know – (*He looks to* BOY.)

MOTHER (*beat*). You know you really do amaze me. Whenever we find a topic, no matter how remote, you find a way to bring it all back to this. So let me tell you now – I don't see any problems with it. He's playing.

FATHER (*still and cold*). He hasn't put that mermaid doll down for weeks. He's a boy.

MOTHER. Yes, darling, I think we can all see that. (*Pause.*) She means a lot to him, he plays with her more than he plays with other children. We can't take that away from him.

Mermaid theme softly plays.

BOY. *A friend to sirens, salt crystalising in my hair like diamonds, I watched them endlessly. Watched them dance their aquatic waltz from crimson sunset to the birth of day. A relationship locked in my retinas. I want to be with them. I want to be with her.*

FATHER. I'm not comfortable with any of it. The mermaid goes.

He puts an arm around MOTHER *and she reluctantly leans in.*

Scene Four

Boy's Room/Jungle

A visual representation of the monologue happens on stage as if we're in his head. Use lighting, puppets, whatever you can.

BOY. Where's my mermaid? I can't find her?

MOTHER. Never mind, darling, we'll look for her tomorrow.

BOY (*deadpan*). School was bad today James was mean to me again but that's okay because his hair looks like mac and cheese I didn't punch him though Dad said I should punch him. Square under the jaw so he bites through his tongue. Mom, am I weird?

MOTHER. My darling, no. No. Of course you're not weird. You are so wanted and so loved, you have no idea.

BOY (*aside*). Never the answer to the question I asked. The worst trait in people. Do we need to get back on that bloody plane and I'll explain that one?

MOTHER. Your father, he, he means well he just… he's never had a son before now, has he, hmm?

BOY. But you've never had a son either.

MOTHER. Ah, yes, Well, I'm a mother. Mothers are quite different to fathers. It's in us, you're part of us. In your head there is a little antenna, and that antenna connects straight up to mine, did you know that? Just tune into me and I'm there.

She kisses his head and tucks him in.

Now try and get some sleep, it's another early day tomorrow and it'll be a better one.

BOY. Do you promise?

MOTHER. Of course I promise. Na-night god bless.

She strokes his hair.

BOY. Mom?

MOTHER. Yes...

BOY. Please...

Fade down to dimmed lights on the instrumental of 'Over the Rainbow'. MOTHER *does not sing it this time and her words are replaced with music. A faint splash of water is heard like a fish swimming away.*

Light up on BOY *awake in bed. Jungle theme. He climbs the set once more and interacts as it comes alive.*

(*Energised.*) It was harder to see the mermaids again after that. I told myself they moved lagoons for whenever I would visit them, the lavender water lay still and the moon forgot to shine as if she was melancholy the sun has failed to kiss her good morning after a long night of shining just for her. But. I had other places to go. I still had my playgrounds. *That's where you'll find me.* Sliding down the vines of trees and swimming between the canopy-top stars each of them with their own stories to tell. The parakeets sing in symphonies, the birds of paradise and their colours melt across an ever-expanding emerald dreamscape. I'd laugh for hours amongst ferns, the waterfalls whimsically quarrel as tigers roar, fireflies flourish and the cicadas hum me to sleep with a lullaby locked in the harmonics of their wings. Hours of navigation through the constellation in my mind. This feeling was golden.

A brief spell of gold light. BOY *smiles. Immediate click into next scene.*

Scene Five

Parents' Evening/Murder in a Classroom

MOTHER, FATHER *and* MRS WHITEMAN *are sat in an office-like manner, the bed once more serving as a table.* BOY *sits side-stage alone again, clearly not within the room.*

MRS WHITEMAN. He does seem to be struggling more and more at the moment, yes. *Eight*-year-olds are rarely interested in school work. This normally is a difficult age when their own minds start to kick in.

FATHER. Is that what we're calling it?

MRS WHITEMAN. He has interests the problem is they're usually off-topic. For example, he loves drama class and RE. He can recite entire Bible stories back to me in a way so honed and specialised you'd think he was actually there himself.

On the other hand his academic work in other areas is the lowest I've ever seen. He struggles to keep up with the whiteboard.

BOY *(aside)*. In my defence the woman wrote like a supercomputer on crack. The squeaking of that pen along the surface would have caused sparks after too long. No wonder she had arthritis. I think she's dead now.

FATHER. He's also mentioned bullying?

MRS WHITEMAN. Bullying yes, well, I haven't seen anything myself that he hasn't been the… Well, bullying isn't a word we'd use, but there are occasional outbursts he seems to be the common cause of. It's quite clear he's struggling socially. I know we spoke briefly about his reaction to physical contact after his incident with James.

MOTHER. He doesn't like being touched.

FATHER. By anyone except –

BOY (*aside*). James never washed his hands after going to the bathroom and his pencils on the desk were always out of line. He was clearly a psychopath.

FATHER. That's not quite how he explained it to us, we'll talk to him, thank you, Mrs Whiteman.

MRS WHITEMAN. How is his emotional perception at home, does he read others well?

MOTHER. Well, yes, I think so.

FATHER. What?

MOTHER. He knows what's going on I think but we have been told he may have a few issues in terms of emotional reception, yes. He doesn't quite feel things the way he should sometimes. He doesn't relate to others well.

MRS WHITEMAN. It's just the other day a relative passed away and obviously I didn't tell my class of eight-year-olds about that… but well, he…

The four actors shift into a classroom set-up with the ensemble joining them. MOTHER *and* FATHER *become classmates with their backs to the audience,* BOY *joins them.* MRS WHITEMAN *stands upstage facing down like a teacher teaching a class. Projection to the back acts as a whiteboard. This scene is fast and should work to 60bpm on the soundscape.*

(*Acting entirely normally.*) And that is why Henry VIII dismantled the Catholic Church, now, if we all turn to page thirty-four.

BOY. Mrs Whiteman?

MRS WHITEMAN. Yes, what is it?

BOY. Are you alright? You seem upset.

MRS WHITEMAN. I'm fine, I, why would you say that? I, never mind, please turn to page thirty-four.

BOY spins in his chair to face downstage. From his trunk he pulls an old-fashioned teacher's pointer for the whiteboard. The remaining cast do not acknowledge him. BOY stands on random trunks to tell his story.

BOY. She said she was fine but everything around her added up to something else. I may not be able to do long division without getting distracted but surely everyone can see that?

Can't they?

As he talks, the teacher replays what he says and bullet points appear on the whiteboard. The scene quickens as it progresses, laser pointers to each evidence-mark fade up across the theatre.

Ten a.m. she enters the classroom and slightly trips on the rug. That rug has always been there. It's *her* rug.

Ten-oh-four she missed Georgia off the register.

MRS WHITEMAN. Guy?

FATHER/GUY. Here.

BOY. You missed Georgia!

MRS WHITEMAN. So I did, Georgia?

MOTHER/GEORGIA. Here!

BOY. Ten thirty-two she started the class two minutes, exactly a hundred and twenty seconds late. She was never late. Ten forty-one spelled 'Morning' M–O–U–R–N–I–N–G on the whiteboard. Ten fifty-seven checks her phone under the desk, you can tell because the light slightly illuminated her glasses enough to see a brief moment of reflection as the Nokia screen danced across her lenses. Eleven twenty-eight a.m.

dismisses us exactly a hundred and twenty seconds early for breaktime, remains behind in the classroom despite it being chocolate biscuit day. Those are her favourite. She said those were her favourite. You remember people's favourite things. That and carrot cake which is gross. She has no taste.

GEORGIA/MOTHER. Miss, it's chocolate biscuit day!

MRS WHITEMAN. I'll be along in a moment, carry on now, don't forget your hats.

BOY. We return from playtime. Murder scene. Exhibit A: coffee cup still on desk exactly where she left it approximately seventy degrees from her untouched pile of papers. Coffee mug empty, kettle remains by the sink untouched. Exhibit B: whiteboard hasn't been rubbed down from last lesson. It's always rubbed down from the last lesson to hide her spelling mistakes. Exhibit C: new addition to attire: small scrunched-up tissue being held to wrist by watch strap. Watch is on time. D: slightly messy hair on the right side of her head indicating a phone has been held. E: phone charger attached to rear desk plug. F: nail on left-hand index finger where immaculate polish once stood is now chipped, bitten. G: ever so slight red mark on right side of face, she's been leaning on it. H: pigeon hole remains empty no papers collected from staff room.

Clearly this is a woman who's falling apart at the seams.

Miss, are you okay?

MRS WHITEMAN. Yes I'm fine sit down for goodness' sake.

BOY. Snappy – a common response to hidden emotions. She shakes her hands as if trying to get water off of them and sniffs. Emma Thompson in *Love Actually* dealing with the grief of her husband cheating. Why is she lying? People shouldn't lie, the truth is always there dotted across the room like a blood spatter analysis if you look closely enough.

Previous set-up of the scene resumes.

MRS WHITEMAN. He brought me a slice of carrot cake the next day.

MOTHER. For some reason he was adamant it was your favourite.

BOY. How's that for poor emotional perception?

Scene Six

Parents' Bedroom

Furniture once more is arranged in a way to resemble a bed.

MOTHER. You shouldn't have told him to punch that child.

FATHER. He didn't really do it.

MOTHER. He bloody did.

FATHER. It's just a bit much, isn't it.

MOTHER. A bit much. What part of what that teacher said sounded even remotely normal to you? Is it any wonder there's bullying going on. Do you think maybe you could spend some more time with him? Get to know him – maybe that'll help things along. The social development and –

FATHER. Oh don't be daft, you know as well as I do the boy isn't interested.

MOTHER. Well, I don't think that's actually true.

FATHER. Listen, I've tried and the boy doesn't want to know. Doesn't even let me touch him.

MOTHER. What you've done is try it your way. He doesn't like football, he doesn't like rough and tumble, he doesn't like army men. You've got to bend to him a little more.

FATHER. Bend any more and you'll snap.

MOTHER. Has it ever crossed your mind that's because I'm doing this entirely alone. Trying to work out exactly what I'm meant to do without any kind of input from my husband.

FATHER. Don't bring that into this.

MOTHER. Alright – from his father.

FATHER. Do you know what he was wearing when I picked him up from Kath's the other night? Do you, huh?

MOTHER. Oh god, you are unbelievable you know – *this* is not about *that*.

FATHER. Isn't it? Cuz I'd say you're looking for problems in all the wrong places.

MOTHER. Well, I know you're hardly bothered about his health.

FATHER. Course I'm bothered about his health. Do you think this is all about him? What about me? What about us? As a father – what I want out of him. D'you think this is how I pictured it?

MOTHER. He needs help. I'm sorry that isn't what you imagined, what are you? Henry VIII? Christ.

FATHER. *Do you know* what he was wearing the other day when I picked him up from Kath's? A dress. A dress. Him and Kath's daughter were in dresses.

MOTHER. Are you implying I'm trying to make him gay? Is that it? Is that what this is about?

FATHER. Leave it, Helen.

MOTHER *puts on a lab coat, steps to centre stage and delivers a short monologue as if at a medical press conference, a single spotlight on her.*

Gold light swells.

MOTHER. Thank you all so much for attending. The amount of research we have now on this topic matter is absolutely incredible. Just in the last five years, 2017 to 2022, we have discovered that the link between autism and gender non-conformity is as high as forty per cent. Research suggests that those with autism show increased homosexuality, bisexuality and it is vital we continue to push to increase awareness and support about non-gender and non-sexuality conformity within this community. Autistic people remain one of the highest sexually assaulted groups. One study in 2018 in the Netherlands even found that autistic people are three times more likely to be –

She cuts off, the lights switch, she removes the lab coat, she's back in the bedroom.

Nobody is strapping your boy down and putting him in a dress and forcing him to play with mermaid dolls, you are aware of that, aren't you? Kath is a dinner lady, she's not working for some gay conversion camp.

FATHER *puts on a red cap and swaps place with* MOTHER. *Tweets pile up, projected on the backdrop of the house, linking autism and homosexuality to the MMR vaccine.* (*See* The Anti-Vax Conspiracy, *Channel 4*.)

Red light swells.

FATHER *lip-syncs to a mash-up of real-life anti-autism clips from documented sources.*

FATHER *switches back to the scene with* MOTHER.

FATHER. Couldn't hurt for him to have some boy friends though, could it?

MOTHER. I'm happy when he's happy and so should you be. Dressing-up games are frankly the least of my concerns with him.

FATHER. And what are your concerns? Do enlighten me? If you're not concerned he's off in a dream world, flapping his hands about, dressing up in women's clothing round your mate's then I don't know what the red flags are you're seeing?

MOTHER. His health. His happiness. I just want him to be happy. Alright? That's what I'm worried about. Just, oh just for fuck's sake try. Try with him. His way. That schedule waits for no one. Just. Sing him 'Over the Rainbow', okay? Put him to bed and sing to him. Start there.

FATHER (*points remote towards a television somewhere in the room*). Whatever you say.

BOY *screams from offstage*.

MOTHER. Night terrors again.

FATHER (*uninterested*). Mmmm.

Scene Seven

Trying

FATHER *and* BOY *sit on the ground centre stage. Their dialogue is comically timed.*

FATHER. So um, how was school?

BOY. Good.

FATHER. And er, are you making friends?

BOY. No.

FATHER. Nice nice. Have you been practising your football?

BOY. No, kicking a ball around the ground seems pointless.

FATHER. Well, the goal is to win, son.

BOY. Then what?

FATHER. Well, then, then you've won, haven't you?

BOY. What do you win?

FATHER. We can't always win *something,* sometimes it's the playing that counts, isn't it?

BOY. The ball hurts my feet and I don't like the mud. It gets on my clothes and makes them dirty and it's cold and feels gross on my skin. Mr Hopkins said I should try harder in PE. But I don't particularly care because he is yet to discover deodorant.

FATHER. Well, maybe he's right, son, eh? Give it a go? You might enjoy it.

BOY. No.

FATHER. Well. That… that ended that idea then, didn't it?

BOY. Yes.

Beat.

FATHER. How about we go to watch the football then? Aston Villa are playing this weekend.

BOY. I'm busy.

FATHER. You're eight years old, son, how can you be busy?

BOY. I'm waiting outside for the cats and dogs this weekend. I want a pet. I've asked you for one but you said no so I'm getting one by other means and any means I see necessary.

FATHER. What? You can't just take someone's dog, mate.

BOY. No, it's going to rain them and I am having a corgi.

FATHER. Rain them? Like, from the sky you mean?

BOY. Mom said it would be raining cats and dogs.

FATHER. She meant heavy rain, son.

BOY. No.

No no.

No. Raining cats and dogs.

FATHER. Don't take her so literally, it can't rain cats and dogs, can it? Ey? When have you ever seen it rain cats and dogs before?

BOY. I haven't but nobody ever said that before and I've got my new welly boots ready. (*He runs over to a trunk and removes a pair of pink wellies with mermaids on them.*) Welly boots!

FATHER. Jesus Christ um, lovely, pick those out did you?

BOY. Mom helped, though my choice is impeccable.

FATHER. Your? Your choice is what, my lad?

BOY. Impeccable.

FATHER. That's a big big word, isn't it. Wouldn't you rather have gotten some army ones?

BOY. No. I'm not an army sort of guy.

FATHER. I, okay... so how about that game, hey?

BOY. No it's going to rain cats and dogs so you won't be able to go anyway, not unless you plan on watching a poodle get kicked across a field into a goal.

FATHER. Look, when people say 'raining cats and dogs' they don't mean there's going to be real cats and dogs actually falling from the sky, they mean it's going to rain heavily. You know when Mom says 'Up the apples and pears,' she means stairs, don't you? Or when someone says 'I'll be five minutes' they mean five hours. Or when someone says get married have kids you'll love every second...

BOY (*pointing happily*). Welly boots.

FATHER. Okay, well, maybe next time then, son? Are you sure you don't want to go see Aston Villa play?

BOY. Yes, the last time I went the cheering was so loud and orange it distracted me from my book. The grounds smelled like testosterone and chips. They don't mix well.

FATHER. Well, it's a game, son, you watch it, you don't read. Orange?

BOY. Like loud. Orange. Orange is loud.

FATHER *freezes*.

Orange IS loud. What I meant by that was that when my senses get overloaded with something in a good or bad way colours show up uninvited like Boris Johnson at a theatre. Going to a football game to me was like being crammed into a tin can with a bunch of stale old men in matching costumes to cheer and watch a ball fly about a field miles away while you try and breathe through the Lynx Africa-filled air. It was primal. But gold is good. Gold is rare. I like people and things that make me see gold. Gold is when I got the part in the school play. I was Peter Pan. Stepping out in front of all the moms and dads under the lights was like stepping into an aurora. A feeling of wholeness. Mrs Whiteman said if I keep it up –

FATHER. Another time then, ay. Would you like me to put you to sleep tonight? Mom's going to be home a little later than usual and I know you like your... your routines and that.

BOY. Do you know 'Over the Rainbow'?

FATHER. No, I don't know that one, son.

BOY. I'll compromise and go to bed later to have Mom.

FATHER. Okay. (*He goes to exit.*)

BOY. Dad?

FATHER. Yes, son.

BOY. Are you going to come and watch – (*Beat.*) the school play?

FATHER. I have to work late, your mom and Aunty Kath will be there.

Long painful beat.

BOY. But –

I'm Peter Pan –

And, don't you like my welly boots? You sniffed and moved your eyes funny when I showed you.

FATHER. They're nice, son, yeah.

Scene Eight

Mother's Monologue

MOTHER *stands alone. She makes a cup of tea or washes up. Blank stage.* MOTHER*'s theme plays. As she talks, shadows arise on the back wall of the house showing the perfect family lifestyle.*

MOTHER. They say being a mother is a calling. In my case it was a call I'd waited my entire life for. Like a mystery Amazon parcel you're waiting, pressed up against the window to arrive, not knowing what you'll get but just knowing in your entire soul that whatever it is; boy, girl, anything – you're going to love it with every fibre of your being. This isn't a feel-sorry-for-me moment. God knows the autism scene has heard enough from moms about that but sadly he never came with instructions and I do think that's important to say. This was a little – (*Beat.*) person. They never tell you that, do they? You're not having a baby. You're having a person. It's not an IKEA flat-pack arriving in the post. And you've got to raise it. He may have galaxies whizzing around in his head and entire planets to call his own, but he is *my* world. Again the thing with worlds is, they're never perfect. There're wars, famines, protests and problems as well as beauty and grace, but with love, they flourish. We all need a little more of that in the world, don't we? Love. The unjudgemental kind, the unconditional kind. Seeing that weary little head fall asleep on my dressing gown was something so special all the poets in the world would have writer's block trying to pull it onto the paper. I'm not saying I made the right choices always, you can't, can you? This is the nineties and we're all just working it out. You couldn't hop on Twitter or YouTube and ask anyone else. What I'm saying is, I tried my best with him, explored every angle. Autism discourse needs to remember that today. Those little chocolate-button eyes and velvet hair are the best delivery a person could have wished for, but with every day he learns to deal with a world not built for him, I learn too. Through that antenna, I'm always tuning into him and trying

to see the world through kaleidoscope eyes. The right
balance of allowing him to escape into those worlds and
knowing he can't live in them forever. (*Desperate*.) Fuck. He
can't live in them forever. A great tightrope act always
balancing imagination and reality, never letting one side get
a fraction too heavy and throw him off-course. Every second
he grows a little older is the moment I feel like I've just
nailed the last chapter. He doesn't see it but as he learns, I
learn, the pat on the back from the universe to say 'you did
today right, Mum,' the pot of gold at the end of my rainbow.

*A flash lights up the shadows on the back wall, as if for a
family photo.* MOTHER *exits.*

*The stage glows temporarily gold, then orange, then fades
down.*

Scene Nine

Dinner/Circus

MOTHER, FATHER, BOY *and* THOMAS *are at the table. The
trunks are arranged in a kitchen dining table set-up.* MOTHER
is serving dinner to the family.

MOTHER. Right, that's yours and this one is yours, Thomas –
(*She places a plate in front of* THOMAS.) and yours,
darling, is just coming.

BOY. We're late on dinner tonight.

MOTHER. It can't always be at the same time, darling, things
come up, don't they.

*They all switch quickly to sitting-on-a-train positions, as a
TFL announcement plays.*

FATHER. Ladies and gentlemen, welcome on board this TFL
service to London Euston, we apologise to each and every one

of you who missed your trains today due to the lack of scheduling. We didn't feel it was important to have any kind of routine and will be taking no responsibility for any inconvenience on getting to work we may have caused you or your aide you wanted to fondle forgetting there was CCTV.

Dinner scene resumes.

You know what the doctors told you, you've got to learn to be more adaptable and face changes.

BOY. The *Titanic* didn't have a routine for their evacuation.

MOTHER (*flustered as she hands him his plate*). Well, the only icebergs present today are the lettuce leaves on your plate. C'mon now let's get some perspective – (*She takes her seat.*)

FATHER. Aren't you eating?

MOTHER. I, well, no I, I didn't feel like cooking three different meals – (FATHER*'s name is crackled.*) tonight, I'm not hungry, now dig in before it goes cold.

FATHER. For goodness' sake, you've got to eat something.

BOY. Ew what's this? My egg isn't runny.

FATHER. You like eggs, just eat it up now come on – (*He turns his attention to* MOTHER.) C'mon you've got to eat something.

MOTHER. I'm not hungry now come on can we just...

BOY. And I don't like beans.

FATHER (*his tone getting harsher*). You DO, eat them. (*To* MOTHER.) Here, love, have some of mine.

THOMAS. Mom, can I have some ketchup?

MOTHER. Yes, darling, I'll just get it.

FATHER (*harshly, losing his temper*). You, sit down.

MOTHER. No it's no problem – (*She gets up to retrieve ketchup.*)

FATHER. Thomas, you go and get it.

MOTHER (*pulling ketchup from her trunk*). There you are, darling.

FATHER. Boys, what did your last slave die of, eh? Darling, could you pass me the salt?

MOTHER *passes* FATHER *the salt.*

MOTHER Now. (*Slight cough.*) How was everyone's days?

THOMAS. Good I –

BOY *stands on the table, unnoticed by his family, as he delivers the monologue and the stage reflects it. The family pull puppet dragonflies from under the table.*

BOY. Mrs Whiteman took us down to the school pond to catch some pondlife for our life-cycle class project. I caught five dragonfly nymphs, did you know that they spent most of their lives underwater before turning into a dragonfly?

Mermaid theme plays.

They have so many colours –

Rainbow lights pulse, nobody notices them but BOY.

– but the babies have pincers that are really sharp and they devour all other pond life and everyone is really scared of them. And then there's the May bug that only gets to live for a day but it is the most exquisite day you could possibly imagine. To live and thrive and blossom and soar and fly and flourish in the space of just twenty-four small hours feeling that liberation and freedom before it all comes crashing and –

FATHER. Your brother was talking.

MOTHER. That's lovely, we have to wait for people to finish speaking though before we start, remember? Thomas, how was your day?

THOMAS. Good.

FATHER. Now look what you've done, Tom, go on, son, you tell me about your day.

THOMAS. We did maths.

BOY. That doesn't sound fun.

FATHER. Shut up. Stop being rude.

BOY. I wasn't being rude.

FATHER. Don't answer back, darling, you've got to tell him.

They freeze except BOY.

BOY (*aside*). Rude is so complicated. If someone asks a question, I answer it. If someone isn't specific with instruction I'll just do as they say. For example: 'Could you take the bins out?' Well, I could but – (*Shrugs.*) Yeah I can do that. I'm capable of that. Oh. Wait. You meant 'WILL you take the bins out for me?' I see. Well. Actually I don't because that's not what you said. *Will* you implies a question of task, *Could you* implies a query of possibility. Say what you mean. D'you see? I just want to be involved.

Dinner resumes.

MOTHER (*her tone raised, on the verge of tears*). It doesn't matter, come on, everyone, just eat your dinner.

FATHER. If I have to sit at this table one. More. Time whilst your mother cries I swear to god.

BOY. I didn't DO anything.

FATHER. Look. At. Me.

BOY *turns his head to make eye contact with his* FATHER *and the stage light pulses red, the lighting shifts and slightly flickers for the first time.*

Do not upset your mother d'you hear or you'll have no dinner. Do you understand me?

BOY. Yes, you're speaking English.

FATHER. What, did you say?

MOTHER. He thinks you mean, no, honey, your father is asking if you appreciate what he's saying.

BOY. Oh yes, yes I do, I'm sorry, Dad.

Beat.

I don't like eggs.

FATHER. RIGHT – (*In total anger he grabs* BOY*'s plate, gets up and throws it offstage.*) You'll go hungry then, won't you.

The red light falls away making the kitchen normal once more. BOY *takes his dragonfly puppet and holds it tightly.*

Silence.

MOTHER, FATHER, BOY, *and* THOMAS *position themselves in a line across the stage with* MOTHER *central,* BOY *left,* FATHER *right,* THOMAS *next to him.*

For your entertainment, ladies and gentlemen, this evening, the moment you've all been waiting for, My wife's famous juggling act.

Soft circus music plays and gets progressively louder as the scene goes on. The monologue quickens in speed. MOTHER *removes a juggling ball from her pocket and begins to slowly toss it up and down.*

MOTHER. Husband. Lover. Worker. I'm devoted to him. Maintain the relationship, keep the romance going. Keep the spark alive. Difficult that when you're running out of oxygen yourself. I've often wondered why we call it a 'spark' in a relationship? Sparks cause fires, don't they? But I'm on hand with the extinguisher whenever one does begin to burn. That temper is new by the way. Never used to be there.

FATHER *tosses her another ball and she catches it, two-ball juggling commences.*

Next. My son, he, well, he has needs. For him a non-runny egg on a plate is like the North Koreans decided to push their border slightly more south. (*She laughs.*) Tiny little things make him uneasy. Lack of routine. Too much routine. Routine in general actually. We all want our kids to do well, don't we, but I'm searching for the needle in a haystack alone sometimes just trying to find my way onto the right road. But with love he'll get there.

BOY *tosses her a ball, she begins juggling with three.*

Then there's Thomas, sweet and dear little Thomas. A child of few words and often overshadowed. Battling every day to show him that there's beauty in the quiet things. Tommy Tickle Mouse I call him, ever so shy and kind. A beautiful April shower to his brother's stunning summer typhoon. I refuse to let one be in the shadow. They're both little stars. Then there's packed lunches, school dinners, homework, laundry, cooking, cleaning, planning, birthdays, Christmas.

They each throw her a ball, she's now juggling with six.

By the time you get to yourself. You haven't got any hands left, you spend all day juggling everyone else that when you try not to drop your own ball…

She attempts to grab an seventh ball from her pocket.

She fails. All balls hit the ground.

Your hands are full.

Scene Ten

Therapy

The same set-up as previously with trunks arranged like a doctor's office, however this time BOY, *visibly older, sits on one too.*

DOCTOR. Tell me more about these colours?

BOY. Every object has a colour, doesn't it, part of the object's soul. When you look at it, it shines like stars and if you don't like it –

He clicks his fingers and the stage lighting changes. Nobody notices this but him.

– then you change it. Of course emotions have colours too. Angry is very red, happy is very gold but very rare, pink is very lovely, there's so *so* many.

DOCTOR. And do you think that everyone can do this? Or just you?

BOY. What do you mean?

DOCTOR. Well, I see this room as grey and there's a sign over there that's sort of blue, isn't there?

BOY. Yes.

DOCTOR. So, we see the room the same, don't we?

BOY. No because that sign isn't blue, it's yellow now.

Lighting change nobody notices. BOY *freezes.*

DOCTOR. How is his socialisation? Any improvements?

MOTHER. Oh yes, some, a lot.

DOCTOR. And still no mention of this to friends, parents, that kind of thing?

MOTHER. No – But he is improving, he still plays imaginary a lot. Just without really moving the toys – you know. Sort of just watches them, moving his hands.

DOCTOR. Pretend play is part of development, this is just a little delayed, that's all. I do however think it's best the other children remain unaware. Children are cruel and studies show the best modes of improving socialisation are to encourage –

MOTHER. Lies?

DOCTOR. Normalcy.

MOTHER. Surely he shouldn't hide it?

Lighting switch.

DOCTOR. Here's the problem and the reality combined into one and the hard-hitting truth – children like him grow up into adults like him. What's cute now won't stay that way. The statistics of unemployment, suicide, abuse and reliance you wouldn't believe. Did you know autistic adults are thirteen times more likely to commit suicide? Have the highest unemployment rate of any group? Have a homeless population the size of… It may all be rainbows to him now but, it won't be. You want him to work, to live… get married, don't you?

DANIEL *enters with* BOY, *a slower version of 'Over the Rainbow' plays. They dance slowly,* MOTHER *watches, before the lights fade down and they exit.*

MOTHER. It isn't all rainbows to him now.

DOCTOR. – in time; he'll become overwhelmed in a world simply not designed for him. What are you going to do? Redesign it? You want him to have a shot, don't you? It isn't too late for him, we *can* help him blend. You said yourself – he wants a career in performance or –

MOTHER. I just don't think –

DOCTOR. There's ways now. Ways we never had before. All those nightmares, the colours, the scary daydreams, the poor communication, the anxiety. We can improve it. Let's try him, trial and error. But with the right combination of the therapy I suggested and trial and error –

MOTHER. He's not a guinea pig.

DOCTOR. No. But sometimes we have to take a gamble. Essentially we want to get him functional. It's a good thing. The goals of ABA are to allow him to associate the abnormal with negative and the normal with positive. The more autistic behaviours he sees as negative, the less likely he is to repeat them. It's very simple. Reward and punishment, reward and punishment until reward becomes more appealing. With medication and dedication there is a huge success rate for… normal life. Career, children, a family.

DOCTOR *and* BOY *freeze,* MOTHER *takes centre stage.*

MOTHER. The snap decision, the balancing of right and wrong in a *great tightrope act*. Try to change your child. It sounds awful, doesn't it.

Long beat, so long it's slightly stifling.

What would you have done?

Another long beat. Circus music resumes but becomes more haunting.

What you have to understand is though his inner worlds were colours and carousels the outer world terrified him beyond all belief. It wasn't all fun and games. So much of it was terrifying. A fish out of water. He was a like a light bulb hooked up to a mass generator, shining so brightly but constantly burning out with dramatic effects. Screams in the night, screams in the day, holding his hair back as he vomited every morning from nerves about going out there into the real.

On the other hand, changing a child. That needs no monologue in a theatre, does it? No.

This would be a very simple world if choices were easy. You can't know what that choice is until you have to make it. You just can't. He'll know that one day. You have to pick and pray you picked right. I watch the television, I see the *Little Britain* era unfolding around us, I hear the parents' comments... I can take them. I love him. But I won't always be here. I don't know if one day he'll be able to stand it.

DOCTOR *and* BOY *unfreeze.*

DOCTOR. A decision please, I'm a very busy man.

MOTHER. We can try.

DOCTOR. Good. Those flapping, flicking, tapping behaviours you said are quite frequent? If so, discourage those. He can start by sitting on his hands at school.

BOY *pulls a chain and padlock from his pocket that he places down on stage. The chain will function as a necklace and must have a padlock on it that can glow in shades of rainbow.*

Just try it.

BOY *(aside walking to centre stage).* My mother never did discourage that. I didn't need her to. Everyone else did it for me. Imagine a great big ball of energy inside you that needs to come out in any way it can. An elevated, exquisite joy that is unrestrainable and unrelatable. Like your soul dancing out of your limbs in a waltz with the world around you. Like conducting water –

As he does this, water projections move behind him like fountains, the stage again comes alive.

– flying through skies and diving into oceans of bliss. Like you can't contain the fauna growing into a botanical garden your body has become. I remember being seven years old and being caught by my teacher. She made me sit on my hands. Locked doors became a big part of my life from then on. I thought that was helping me. I was in my twenties when I learned we've created a generation of prepubescent pressure cookers. Other people do this too. Not in the same way but that there are so many of us with fireballs in our chests burning up until we taste sulphur in our mouths and swallowing it back down to please the dinner-party dynasty of the world. I believe there are hurricanes sat behind hazel eyes, cosmoses kept captive in coping and personas prisoners to patriarchy. This world, seeing who we are – is rare. Any scrap of difference or non-conformity to what the world expects you to be – chewing on it and tonguing it like a cut in your mouth over and over instead of spitting it out, breathing and just being exactly who you –

The DOCTOR, *unseen until now, places the necklace around* BOY*'s neck, clicks it into place and visibly places the key into his pocket.*

– are.

Blackout except the glow of the necklace.

Scene Eleven

Boy's Bedroom

Trunks are arranged like a bed once more. BOY *sits upon them. His necklace shining.*

BOY (*closing his eyes and straining*). Jungle – (*He opens them, nothing.*) JUNGLE – (*He opens them, nothing.*) JUNGLEEEEEEEEEEEE – (*Still nothing. He screams.*)

Silence.

(*Closing his eyes and straining.*) Running with Wolves. (*Nothing.*) RUNNING WITH WOLVES. (*Nothing.*)

Silence.

He pulls the necklace off his head. It's loose and slips off. As it comes away the rainbow light on it goes off, the rainbow lamp stage left comes on.

Silence.

Running with WOLVES.

Drumbeat. Upbeat Jungle theme.

Overjoyed screams from BOY.

Drumbeats quicken as an incredibly powerful melody sets in. The music swells into a joyous symphony. BOY *runs on the spot as the screen and stage around him come alive and burst into a forest of colours. Use puppetry, lighting or any means necessary to transform the stage into the other world. The music key changes and swells. He jumps into the air and the scene shifts to flying with dragons, he climbs the set, smoke bellows from it with dragons' roars heard. At the music's most powerful moment, holographic planets, mermaids and dragons fly around the stage. He puts the lock back around his neck. All lights end. The stage is dull, the rainbow shines in the necklace. He's in his bed alone. Blackout.*

Scene Twelve

Army

Entire cast enter.

MOTHER. He doesn't like army men.

FATHER. Troops. Time to learn how to blend into an
environment. You've all got your camo. Good. (*He looks to*
BOY.) EYES FORWARD, SOLDIER.

A red light pulses as the FATHER *stares into* BOY*'s eyes.*
He continues to walk the line.

In the field this leads you to be undetectable to the enemy.
Hides you. It's a dangerous world out there. You have to
camouflage into your background so you don't stand out. So
you survive.

An entire movement sequence happens reminiscent of an
army training drill to a music score. (Inspired by Cavetown's
'Boys Will Be Bugs'.) Use pieces of the set, lighting and
projection to convey the massive physical struggle to become
the societally accepted idea of normal. It should be an
uncomfortable sequence, dropping in and out of army drills
and doctors' offices, but clearly reminiscent of
ABA/conversion therapy. Examples include BOY *walking*
with sweets and having them switched out to a pill bottle
without his noticing. The sequence should follow the tone of
the rest of the imagination sequences before it, fun, fast but
with majorly sinister undertones. It should also show an
ageing-up of BOY *in his movement. All autistic body*
language to have dropped by its end. During the sequence
the cast change BOY *out of his clothes and into ones much*
more like theirs, they gel his hair in the same style, he now
matches them in every way.

FATHER *makes firm eye contact with* BOY, *the stage glows*
red but BOY *holds* FATHER*'s gaze.*

How'd you feel?

BOY. I don't.

Sir.

FATHER. Good.

FATHER *exits*.

BOY *attempts to pull the necklace off his neck over his head as he did before. It no longer fits easily but with strain it comes away, it flickers on and off for a moment before dying. He sits centre stage alone. Again, a visual representation of his monologue is shown behind him, using shadow puppets.*

BOY. I want to run away sometimes, but my feet just can't take me. But my mind can still. Just about. As it always did. My brain escapes to a Victorian theatre on a rainy night. Candle lights flicker in the windows as the storm lashes down outside relentlessly.

Thunder crash. He winces then stops himself.

A vast open auditorium where gas lamps flicker and warm down as an orchestra warms up in the pit below. There's a dome painted with the most exquisite artwork you've ever seen and in the centre hangs a chandelier so bright a thousands stars could bicker in jealousy. An actress sits on the oak wood stage, totally alone in a costume befitting of royalty.

MOTHER *enters*.

I sit with her, on the dusty boards and ask what this place is. As the jewels in her crown reflect off the tears on my cheeks I learn of a place so surreal that magic and wonder can exist in simultaneous bliss – a place where oddities and outcasts thrive, where abnormalcy can grow and flourish like the deepest jungle. A place that could only be real over a rainbow.

Beat.

But she's not real.

MOTHER *exits*.

None of it is. She's older than the last time I came, sort of thinner and translucent. Her life is going from her and there's nothing I can do. She doesn't smile so kindly any more and the ceiling is leaking.

Staging changes.

I close my eyes and imagine beams to replace the damage.
Nothing. Every time I close the door to come back to reality
it pushes back a little harder as if to say '*Don't leave us,
don't let us go. Are you really going to walk out on us?*' But
I have no choice. I have a life outside of this one. It's duller.
Colder. More hateful. But it's where I belong. I think I
understand why Dorothy left Oz.

*He puts the necklace back on. It's heavier than before. The
light in it shines again as the rainbow lamp dies. He holds in
tears. Blackout.*

Scene Thirteen

Man Up/School

BOY *sits upon the trunks arranged like a desk. He pulls papers
from one of them. His necklace shows one bar of rainbow. His
mannerisms are significantly more typical. Comedic timing.*

BOY (*straining to learn*). Anatomy of a man.

The Vitruvian Man appears on the screen behind him.

Jesus here we go. Okay. (*Reading.*) 'Men walk more upwards
than women. Their chests out and crotches forward.'

Right.

He gets up.

Shoulders back – (*He comically pushes his shoulders back.*)
Chest forward – (*He pushes his chest out.*) Crotch forward.
Am I really… Okay fine – (*He pushes his crotch forward
before awkwardly waddling back to the desk.*) Okay now
what. 'Men walk with swagger.' What the actual fuck am I
reading? (*His necklace pulses in full colour.*) Okay fine fine
fine. Swagger. I can do swagger. (*He awkwardly staggers
across the stage and winks.*) Heyyyyyyy. D'you come here

often? I like… cars… and… stuff. Like my aftershave? It's called Tyres and Testosterone. I smell… like…

…a concept…

No flowers for me I want to smell like a junk yard. Yeeaahh. Can I take you out on a drive? Oh this is ridiculous. (*His necklace pulses in full colour once more*.) FINE FINE. (*Continues to read*.) 'Men rarely use first names.' Well, that just seems entirely problematic, doesn't it. 'They refer to reach other as mate, pal, dude or… *sport*?' Good. Okay. Let's try that. Hey, dude, wanna hit the er, gym? Buddy boy? Old pal? Governor? (*Visibly getting more frustrated but we see improvement quickly*.) Hey. Hi. Hello. Hands in pockets right hands in pockets. Hands out of pockets? Hands in pockets. Crotch forward. Shoulders back. Hey man, I was wondering if you wanted to hit the gym. No, that sounds too grammatical. Hey man, I'm going to the gym. Nope, why would I say that, wait to be asked okay. (*Pause*.) Sorry dude, I can't tonight I'm going to the gym, I'll hit you up another time though?

Wow. Okay. That. That was better.

(*Reading*.) 'Men rarely express large passionate opinions. Unless it comes to women or money.' Ay ay aye. Okay. Cool cool cool. I thought *Moulin Rouge* was a brilliantly crafted movie showcasing love exactly as it should be, in glorious ballads set in the heart of Victorian Bohemian Paris.

Eh.

I thought *Moulin Rouge* was a very good movie showing lots of emotions and stuff? Better better.

Hey dude, have you seen *Moulin Rouge*?

Oh, is that the one with Nicole Kidman basically topless? Yeah man, it was okay. SCORE.

(*Reading*.) 'Now blend those elements together.' Now blend them? Blend them? (*His necklace glows slightly*.) Okay okay okay Jesus would you calm down.

I'm trying.

Hey, umm, Abby I wanted to know if you'd maybe go on a date with me? Ehhhhh. Hey Abby, are you busy later? Hey umm Abby would you like to... hang out? Ohh this is painful.

He grabs a backpack from the trunk and begins walking in his new style, less comically more realistically. He puts a bracelet on his wrist.

Hey Abby, would you? Ehh I smell like burn-outs and gasoline I – ?

ABBY *enters.*

ABBY. Hey, are you alright?

BOY. Sure, I'm alright, as opposed to all left, but I am left-handed – and footed cuz I play... football... and...

ABBY. Is that? Aftershave?

BOY. Yes. It's meant to smell kinda musty. But I think I smell like Ann Widdecombe's crotch.

ABBY. I like it.

BOY. Yeah, I agree, dude.

ABBY. What?

BOY. Nothing.

ABBY. You called me dude.

BOY. Dudette.

ABBY. How is that better?

BOY. Good point.

So uh – (*Slightly tics.*) what are you up to this weekend?

ABBY. Actually, me and a few friends are having a sleepover in a few days, would you like to come?

BOY. Oh I wasn't asking for an invite, I didn't know that was an event that was happening I was asking you what you were doing because that's polite and –

ABBY. Of course you didn't know.

BOY. I. I would love to yeah. Thanks for asking.

ABBY smiles back.

It's polite to say thank you when asked places.

ABBY. No problem, it's my birthday but no pressure – (*She laughs.*)

BOY. Sure, I'll bring something along.

ABBY. Awesome! Friday, I'll message you, my address. You're on the group chat, right?

BOY. Uh. No. I'm not. I don't have a phone; I'll use my mom's.

ABBY. Oh, okay, I'll add you! I should probably get going – you know how Miss Boucher is when you're even a second too late. Like honestly, woman, chill, it's just a schedule.

BOY. Ha, yeah, speaking of that, what time is the party, sleepover, thing?

ABBY. Get to mine for around eight-thirty-ish.

BOY. Ish?

ABBY. You're funny. See ya.

BOY. See ya… Abby.

She exits.

Woooo. Okay okay. Cool. (*He looks to his necklace. The rainbow is out. He smiles.*)

Scene Fourteen

Abby's Sleepover

ABBY, EMILY *and* JAKE *are on stage already.*

BOY *enters.*

BOY. Hey, hi.

ABBY. You made it!

BOY. I made what?

ABBY. Thanks for coming.

BOY. You're welcome, this is for you – (*He hands her a present.*)

ABBY. Oh my god, this is incredible, you DREW this? I – never knew you could.

BOY. Hey, everyone.

EMILY. Well, look who decided to join us for once – (*High-pitch laugh.*)

BOY (*aside*). Remember I told you about Emily? That's her. A blessing, truly.

JAKE. Hey. Wow, you wore cologne and a necklace to a sleepover, someone's trying hard, aren't they.

ABBY. Jake, don't be rude. I like the necklace. It's different.

BOY. Thanks.

ABBY. Come sit sit, we're gonna watch a scary movie!

BOY. Sure! Sounds good.

They huddle and face the back screen.

(*Aside.*) It did not sound good. Why the hell would anybody want to make themselves scared? That kind of illogical thinking just doesn't make any kind of sense. Fear is orange and orange is not good. Orange is friends with red, red is anger, pain, suffering – fear is the same thing, it just feels more. Cowardly.

ABBY. You excited? This is *The Zombies have Hepatitis 4*.

BOY. Four. Wow they made more of those. Great.

JAKE. Hope you're not too scared.

BOY. No, I'm fine.

EMILY (*squealing*). Oh my god, Jake, you're SO funny. There's no mermaids in this one though, sorry!

BOY (*aside*). She really was repellent.

JAKE. Mermaids, ay? I was right, pay up, everyone, he is queer. Bad luck, Abby.

BOY. I'm not.

JAKE. Yeah? Look me in the eyes and say that.

BOY (*beat*). I'm not.

ABBY. Stop it, Jake, come on, the zombies are just about to work out how to cook brains al dente...

BOY*'s* MOTHER*'s phone pings, the message shows on screen but nobody notices it but him.*

'Hi Helen, Kate from the PTA here, I was just wondering if you were planning on getting back to me? You've missed twelve meetings in a row now, not great frankly.'

BOY *replies.*

'Hi Kate, sorry, this isn't Helen. I've got my mom's phone for the night, It's me, her son.'

ABBY. EWWW oh my god there's so much brains in this one!!

EMILY. Gross!

JAKE. How you holding up there?

BOY. Good. Fine. Nice... brains.

JAKE. Yup.

Another text message hits the screen.

'Honestly Helen if that's an excuse you expect me to believe it's no wonder your son's a freak is it?'

BOY*'s necklace immediately begins to glow and pulse. Heavy music sets in with a much darker feel.*

BOY. Please no not here no.

ABBY. Everything okay?

BOY. Yes. Yep.

He shoves the necklace down his top.

ABBY. Are you sure you look so...

BOY (*breathing heavily*). I'm fine I just need some –

The scene goes into slow motion, reflected in the sound and lighting, the ensemble lift BOY *for a moment, then the pace picks up again. Like a time warp turned on and off simulating a meltdown in a way that won't make an audience actually have one – no strobe lighting.*

I need some air.

JAKE. Wow, dude, chill out, what's wrong with you?

Light changes.

EMILY. What are you doing stop it, calm down! What is WRONG with you?

JAKE. I told you inviting him was a mistake, can't even handle a horror movie.

The lights surge again. Audio should be uncomfy but not overstimulating for an autistic audience. BOY *fights with the weight of the padlock.*

BOY. I gotta – (*He holds in vomiting.*) I gotta go, Abby.

Lights continue to pulse slowly as BOY *runs.* ABBY, JAKE *and* EMILY *exit. He's running centre stage with a montage of colours on the screen and the stage lighting. This time, dark and terrifying. He fights to pull the lock off his neck but he can't, it's too tight. He keeps running. An electrical-surge noise like a generator overheating. He collapses. Blackout.*

Scene Fifteen

Back on the Airplane

The ensemble rejoin on stage to form the airplane sequence from before once more. This time, BOY *takes the role of hostess.*

BOY. Ladies and gentlemen, we're expecting some mild turbulence on our flight this evening. Please make sure to sit back in your seats, turn off *Shrek 2*, hold onto your armrests, glasses, wigs, dentures and microwaved dinners. I will shortly be passing through the cabin with a friendly selection of whiskey and Xanax, if you're feeling a little jittery – now's the time. Emergency exits are here, here, here and here. In the event of an emergency, masks will drop down from above your heads. An important rule we always forget in life but never in the sky – see to yourself before assisting others. I will have a word with our captains and soon we'll be back in the breezy. In the meantime please enjoy the view – on the left you can see Spain, on the right, the jet engine on fire.

The stage switches to allow BOY *to sit next to* MOTHER *and father, in captain hats.*

You told people.

MOTHER. This is flight 1401 to air-traffic control, can we have confirmation on our position.

BOY. You told people.

FATHER. Prepare for potential emergency landing.

BOY. We're not going to emergency land – I thought it was our secret.

MOTHER. Mind that bird before it becomes lodged in one of our jet engines.

FATHER. Roger that.

MOTHER. Water below?

FATHER. Sharks below.

BOY. Ladies and gentlemen, please place your hands behind your head, keep your knees firmly together and lean forward. And do mind out for your microwaved dinners.

MOTHER (*manic*). Spoiler it really is microwaved!

BOY. Here it comes.

MOTHER. Hold it.

FATHER. Brace!

Ensemble, MOTHER, FATHER *and* BOY *all brace.*

End of Act One.

ACT TWO

Scene One

Entirely black stage. A screen upon the back wall. BOY *sits on a trunk centre stage that is covered with movie stickers and pop-culture references. Another three trunks are placed nearby. A small rainbow neon lamp is on a table stage left. The lamp is not illuminated.* BOY *wears the padlock necklace around his neck with a rainbow light upon it. It is also not illuminated.*

BOY. Who got the worse ending, Peter Pan or Wendy? We'll never really know but that's something I've thought about a lot. Peter got what he'd always wanted – he never had to grow up, but with Hook dead and Wendy gone, I wonder if his world lost a little piece of its shine. Then there's Wendy, she got what she'd never wanted. She returned home, grew up, got married and had children. She chose the mundane over the magical. I could never work out who I felt more sorry for.

Scene Two

Boy's Bedroom

BOY *sits on the bed alone. The necklace dull, the rainbow lamp remains off.*

MOTHER. Can I? Can I come in?

BOY. Yes.

(*Beat.*) I'm sorry.

MOTHER. That's okay. I'm sorry too. Sorry I didn't explain things more and sorry, just sorry you had to see that.

BOY. I just want to be like everybody else... but... You don't
think it's a good idea, do you?

MOTHER. It isn't that I think it's a bad idea. It's that I'm
worried for you. You're doing so well as you are and tonight
was a blip, just a blip. You've kept yourself grounded,
darling. Sometimes it's like we're trying to climb the
Himalayas when we're meant to be on the Yorkshire Dales.
Life isn't easy. But you're strong. You've got it in you,
I know you have.

BOY. I know that if I didn't do as I'm supposed to and acted in
a way that feels right – I wouldn't have friends and parties
and things like that...

MOTHER. I'm sure you would.

BOY. No. I wouldn't. They might not know it but in the
playground at school I stand back and watch them do their
disabled impressions. Copying famous sketch shows. This is
the *Little Britain* era. Its humour, its comedy. We had to read
a book about some boy like me who finds a dead dog on the
grass, and do you know that was the first time in the world I
have ever picked up a book and believed wholeheartedly that
there's a place in the world for people like me and I can't say
so. I can't say so because when class ends literally every
single person makes fun of it. Of him. Of me.

MOTHER. I know –

BOY. Why did you tell people?

MOTHER. We didn't tell people... we... placed our trust in
someone we thought was a family friend. We thought it
would help. We needed someone to talk through it with and
Rachel was that person.

BOY. I. Understand.

MOTHER. Would you – like your song this evening?

BOY (*beat*). No. That's okay.

Scene Three

Pond/School

BOY *walks with his backpack on and sits on the edge of the stage pretending to throw stones into a pond.* ABBY *enters.*

ABBY. Is this seat taken?

BOY. Oh. Hey. No. It's not a seat it's a small rock.

ABBY. I meant can I sit with you please?

BOY. On the small rock?

ABBY. Sure.

BOY. Okay.

ABBY. Can we be here? Down by the pond I mean, in school time?

BOY. If you're asking *can* we be here the answer is yes. If you're asking *should* we be here the answer is no. But also yes. Make sense?

ABBY. You have no idea how much sense that makes.

They sit with their legs overhanging the stage. ABBY *picks up a rock and throws it.*

BOY. Wow careful there you'll hit a mermaid.

ABBY (*laughs*). Imagine. Try not to let Emily get to you.

BOY. I'm serious, there's got to be hundreds in here!

ABBY. You reckon?

BOY. Psh, sure. That and at least a million teachers' hopes and dreams. And I think – that's part of a shopping trolley. And that... that looks like –

ABBY. The cucumber from Sex Ed.

BOY. I was gonna say lunch but sure.

ABBY (*laughs*). You're actually really funny.

BOY. Yeah I get that a lot.

They make eye contact for a moment and smile before pulling away.

ABBY. Wow, um dragonflies. There's lots of uh, dragonflies – (*Pause.*) I've never sat here long enough to notice them, look there's a purple one! And green!

BOY. We used to come down here fishing as kids with Mrs Whiteman, remember?

ABBY. Oh my god that's right! You knew like every bug on the planet, didn't you?

BOY. Sure did, not exactly a turn-on that, is it. I don't know anyone who's ever gotten laid because they know the entire cast of *A Bug's Life* on a personal level.

Beat.

ABBY. So is it true they only live for a day? After they leave the water, I mean?

BOY. No, that's the May fly. But I'm sure dragonflies don't have it perfect; they spent all their life up until today under water. Suppose they took a risk. Wanted a change.

ABBY (*laughs*). What a strange way to look at it.

BOY. You can see anything in any way if you look hard enough, there's colours all around us. Even the water is alive. Here – (*He picks up another rock.*) you've gotta get the angle right to make them bounce. Let me show you – (*He hands her the rock and positions himself behind her holding on her hands as he guides them.*) Hold your arms in a backwards C-shape, yeah, like that. Now look at the water, wait for the perfect stillness. Keep waiting. Keep waiting. Imagine you're aiming for that horizon, pull back and… (*Together they release the rock.*) There! (*As the rock bounces, ripples of colour bounce across the stage.*) Not bad for a first-timer.

ABBY. I'll add it to my CV for college.

They laugh.

BOY. Hey, Abby. There's something I wanted to tell you, about the other night I mean, I'm not sure if the movie was the reas...

ABBY (*interrupting*). Sure. But first, I wanted to say thank you for the gift you got me.

BOY. It was nothing really I wanted to tell you —

ABBY *leans in and kisses him on the cheek. The whole stage glows gold before fading down. His necklace glows.*

ABBY *stays close to him and plays with his necklace, her glace fixed on it lovingly, she takes a key out of her pocket and holds it in her hand.*

ABBY. Now what was it you wanted to tell me?

BOY. Nothing, nothing really, I just wanted to say I'm sorry again.

A school bell chimes, she grabs him, pulls him up jokingly and then runs to class. She does not exit but freezes halfway on her way out.

(*Erratically, happily picking up pace.*) I did not see that coming and I mean I did not see that coming. I see everything coming. Okay. Woof. I can read a room like a book, see through people like glass, each head nod, eyebrow raise and slight scratch might as well be in bright pulsing neon. A person's intentions might as well be written on their face. I did not see this coming! AHH. I can see everything coming! I can sniff out a lie like a dog, I can see the politics of the school yard like a game of Battleships.

He taps the lock around his neck. It suddenly sparks rainbow. Steps to the back of the stage.

JAKE (*to* ABBY). So we just spent all break looking for you. No sweat. Didn't have to tell us where you were or anything. Not like we're your best mates and we were stressed out of our brains...

ABBY. Would you please shut up?

EMILY. Jake. Quiet – (*She squeals.*)

ABBY. I was actually just hanging out with him, I felt bad after what happened and…

JAKE. With HIM? Oh mermaid boy.

BOY. Truly a pathetic shot.

EMILY. You're so funny, Jake!

BOY. There she comes right on cue – who'd have thought it. One day she's going to take off her running shoes, stick them under her desk and swap into office wear I just KNOW it.

EMILY. Oh, how's he feeling after his complete apocalyptic freakout the other night?

ABBY. Fine I think, he seems fine now.

EMILY. Aw bless, hope he didn't run into a lamppost on his way back to Narnia.

BOY. I'll give her that one, I didn't know literary references to the works of C.S. Lewis were in her wheelhouse.

JAKE. Well… actually, Abby, we saw you two smooching down by the pond. Got anything to tell us, hey? Didn't know gay men were your thing. You know he's gay, right. He moves his hands in that – way – yaknow. Leans into his hip. Talks about how he's figuratively met fucking mermaids.

BOY. Literally not figuratively.

ABBY. No I, er –

EMILY. Go on, Abby, tell us are you in love? Sorry if we cramped your sleepover style the other night! You were getting close under those blankets…

Kissy kissy kissy…

ABBY. I, no –

JAKE. He's cute, Abby, maybe all your kids can have their own weird little rainbow necklaces too.

ABBY. Are you kidding? It wasn't like that it isn't like that. We're just friends, we –

EMILY. Here's the problem and the reality rolled into one. You want to be popular, don't you. Here's your choice. People like him grow up into adults like him and you don't want to be seen around adults like him, right. Your reputation starts here. High school doesn't end. Look at the world, Abby. Look at who's on top. Is it them? No.

JAKE. A choice please.

ABBY. STOP. He's just a friend. He's not even that, he's less than that, it was a sympathy thing, okay. I felt sorry for him are you happy now? I kissed him on the cheek out. Of. Sympathy. Now leave it.

They exit. BOY *watches them do so. Looks sheepish for a second, runs his fingers through his newly gelled hair, looks down at his hands, briefly stims, sighs, and exits.*

Scene Four

The Baby Birds

FATHER *enters: he appears to be packing, though this is not noticed by the audience until the end of the monologue.*

FATHER. When I was young, we used to play out a lot. We were a big family and there were a lot of kids in the area we lived in. It was your sort of council estate that backed onto a nearby woodland. There was none of this 'Watch out for strangers' or 'Don't play in the road' back then. Ten a.m. on a Saturday and the front door was open – off you went to meet your mates. My big brother Charlie was charged with looking after us younger ones but never did.

It was early spring one year and we were down by the river where the old rope swing hung that Charlie was deadly proud of. He'd made it out of a couple of sticks and rope we stole from the farmer's shed over the field and we'd all line up and take turns to fly out over the water below when he told us we were allowed a turn.

I was lining up behind my brothers one day when I heard a helpless little squeak from a nearby bush. A fox, or cat, or maybe even one of us the day before had knocked down a birds' nest made of moss and twigs down from its rest. I reached down and uncovered two little baby birds in the undergrowth. The remaining eggs were all broken and beside them lay a couple of lifeless little bodies and mangle of feathers. They were so small. I went to pick them up but Charlie hit me with a stick. 'What're you doin'?' he yelled and cheered as my siblings and the rest of the gang looked on. 'Leave 'em there. They're dirty and disgusting. Let 'em die, let nature do its thing, Tim.' I looked down at them, helpless and squawking and I just... couldn't. So I picked them up and shoved them in my hoodie pockets. As I ran home I gathered up moss, grass, weeds and plants, clambered up the stairs and I emptied out an old shoe box before placing them gently inside. I'd read in a book you have to feed baby birds every two hours so I did. I mushed up some seeds in milk and every hour or so would give them just a little bit as they looked up at me with those little eyes and beaks open wide. I don't know what happened after that but I woke up the next morning to hear my mother screaming down the house. Charlie and the others had told her already. I reached for my shoe box but it was gone. I'd worked so hard – so hard to keep them alive but I couldn't stay awake long enough.

I never saw them again but I got a good whack round the ear and wasn't allowed back to the woods for a week after that.

All I wanted to do – was look after them and make sure they were okay. I wanted them to have a chance but the point is – the point is –

The point is... this world, is cruel. It's big, it's scary and it's tough. There's no place for the gentle things. It ain't that kindness is a weakness. Nah. It's that life just ain't that kind in itself. If only I'd have left them where they were – just let it be – then I know the same outcome would have happened but maybe, just maybe it would have hurt a lot less.

BOY *enters*.

BOY. So it occurred to me first when I was a child: there's got to be a way to have both. To live in a world of fantasy where gingerbread houses and chocolate streams can flow and yet a suit and tie aren't totally out of place.

Needless to say episodes like Abby's birthday continued to happen and, even less shockingly still, Mom and Dad split but as every day went by I got a little better at blending. I liked to think of myself as a chameleon stuck to the classroom wall or a cuttlefish gliding down the corridors. Thankfully camo was very fashionable by the time I got to college. A secret agent in disguise blending so perfectly to whatever environment he is put in. I took up drama class and decided firmly against every teacher's suggestion I go into something more 'sensible' as a career path. They didn't get it. Why would I want an office job when I can make universes really come to life?

I found it. A way to make the two worlds meet. Nobody can see you – if you're somebody else.

MOTHER. Would you go to bed?

BOY. Yes – sorry.

THOMAS (*from offstage*). Where's Dad?

BOY *gets into bed*.

Scene Five

BOY *stands alone on a blank stage. Audition room chatter is heard in the background.*

BOY. You've gone through this a million times, okay alright. Woo there's so much riding on this. Okay but keep it together. (*His necklace shines and he comically punches it.*) Not now. 'Hi today I'm going to be performing for you.' Okay okay – 'Hi I'm – ' God no why do I sound like that what's wrong with me? Hi. Nope. Hello. No. Bonjour. Absolutely not. Today I'm going to be performing for you. Daarh. I'm going to be... I'm going to be. (*His necklace shines, he notices it.*) Hmm. Oh no. No. You've got to be kidding me if you think you're getting out today. (*He responds to the necklace like he's been given a small electric shock.*)

FEMALE VOICE-OVER. They're ready for you now.

BOY. Okay. Thank you.

Blackout to immediate spotlight on BOY.

Hi, I'm going to be performing for you...

His necklace shines.

Something that I wrote.

And I'm gonna do it... as I get out of this – (*He gestures to his chain.*)

Drumbeats quicken as the same powerful melody from Act One, Scene Eleven sets in. BOY *begins to pull at his necklace in a heavily choreographed movement piece. The stage comes to life by whatever means to show the imagination sequences he had as a child as he pulls and tugs off the necklace telling the stories. This time the light on stage should reflect his complete control over it. The music swells into a joyous symphony as rainbow light bends around, conducted by him, making the illusion of water. With each choreographed tug the fountains of light pulse... He continues to pull at his necklace during choreography until at the music's climax it comes away. (Ideally in one and unbroken.) He stands centre stage, heavy breathing, with the necklace raised above his head. The whole stage, rainbow lamp, trunks and him are lit up in rainbow colours. The necklace is dead.) It is extremely important this scene, as opposed to the others, shows complete masterful control over what once controlled him.*

The colours begin the fade down into just the single spotlight.

Silence.

Thank you.

MALE VOICE-OVER. Will you work overseas?

BOY. Yes.

MALE VOICE-OVER. Will you commit to a year contract?

BOY. Yes.

MALE VOICE-OVER. Any medical conditions that might affect your work?

Brief blackout.

Lights up and the necklace is returned to BOY*'s neck.*

BOY. None.

Blackout.

Scene Six

Circus

BOY *sits centre stage with the trunks arranged around him like a ring, his back to the audience. Powerful music with a circus theme begins, the lighting mirrors that used in the imagination scenes. Rainbow lights pulse. The lamp on the side of the stage lights up.*

MALE VOICE-OVER. And now, ladies and gentlemen, Kyō-Sō's world-famous circus presents, Fragments of Imagination.

Circus music intensifies in an otherworldly way, DANIEL, RACHEL, EMILE, LARA *enter throughout the monologue to position for the start of the show – a circus is assembling in colour around* BOY.

BOY. A world where reality and fantasy could mix. Where you get to live in a world that doesn't exist – this is all I've ever dreamed of. Where fragments of imagination are close enough to pull through the void from that world into this, to breathe, to live and feel whole as the conventions of the real world slip away – where you get to be home and safe forever – *I've fought in great battles, slain dragons and trapezed through my circus in the skies of my mind.*

DANIEL *unfreezes,* BOY *is notably alarmed someone has broken into the freeze frame in his mind. The rainbow lamp lights up.*

DANIEL. Except this is really happening.

BOY. What?

DANIEL. You're here. We're up in three, two –

BOY. Wh...

DANIEL. One.

The freeze frame ends, all of the cast jump forward in slow motion. BOY *stands back a moment before* DANIEL *grabs him by the hand and pulls him forward, a rainbow of light hits the stage. Blackout. The sound of a crowd cheering.*

Scene Seven

The Start

BOY *and* DANIEL *are wrapping up after the show. The trunks are laid out like costume boxes.*

BOY. Hey um, thanks for uh, giving me the nudge by the way –
I'm –

DANIEL. By nudge do you mean heaving your ass onto the stage?

BOY. Yep.

DANIEL *takes a seat on one of the trunks and stares at* BOY *for a moment.*

What?

DANIEL. Nothing. I'm just gonna say I've never seen an act like yours before.

BOY. I don't think many have.

DANIEL. How'd you do it?

BOY. You wouldn't believe me if I told you.

DANIEL. Is that so? So is it like some kinda superpower?

BOY. No. Absolutely not. It's the most normal thing in the world – to me.

DANIEL. Well – you got to take that leap some time. Own it. Whatever it is.

They both freeze.

MALE VOICE-OVER. And now, ladies and gentlemen, our incredible Lara in the trapeze act of –

A projection of LARA *stood on a high-rise platform is shown on screen.*

BOY (*flustered*). So what about you? I mean, tell me about you.

DANIEL. What's to tell? Circus boy through and through.

BOY. Looked like a damn sight more from where I was sitting.

DANIEL. I strap a pair of skis to my feet and jet around on water. Hardly the most impressive thing in the world, is it.

BOY. I think it's kinda cool.

DANIEL. I suppose it is, guess I do it to let the world escape me for a moment.

BOY (*he glances to his lock*). That must be nice.

Beat.

DANIEL. Wanna find out?

BOY. What?

DANIEL. Wanna give it a shot? It's like flying – just… wetter.

BOY. Are you kidding me?

DANIEL. I'm not kidding, c'mon, think of it as an initiation into performance life.

BOY. Maybe.

DANIEL. Maybe doesn't make sense. That's not an answer and you'll see. Come on. Take the leap.

BOY (*his necklace glows*). I'm not so sure.

DANIEL (*extending his hand*). Trust me, I promise you'll be fine.

BOY. You're certain?

DANIEL. Does a bear shit in the woods? Of course I'm certain, now are you coming or not?

DANIEL *exits.*

BOY. Yes! Wait.

The projection of LARA *makes the leap, we don't see if she catches the trapeze.*

Blackout.

Scene Eight

Skiing

BOY *and* DANIEL *enter with a pair of skis each. They both grab a trunk, running excitedly, placing them open and facing towards them at the edge of the stage. From the trunks they pull out a ski-rope wire each, the handle end reels out but the other remains fastened to the trunk. They head to centre stage and sit on the two remaining trunks.*

DANIEL. Right, put your toes in and push down, like putting on a welly boot.

BOY. Should we really be in the ring this late?

DANIEL. Everybody is already half-unconscious at a bar, I think we're fine. Toes in.

BOY pushes his feet into both skis and goes to stand.

Hold on a second. Right. Hold tight to the handle, if you need to, let go. When the motor comes round wait for me to say go, then I want you to stand up in a squat position as if you –

BOY stands up and immediately falls comically over.

(*Heaving him back onto the trunk.*) You okay?

BOY. Uh-huh.

DANIEL. When I say go. Pull back, eyes on the horizon – (*Mimicking* ABBY *and* BOY.) The best way to learn is to be clear. Imagine if an air hostess never told you what to do if the plane went down. Ready?

BOY (*panicked*). I dunno…

DANIEL. Aaaaand… NOW.

The boys immediately pull up to standing and take two smaller puppet versions of themselves from their trunks. The lighting changes to illustrate fast movement as they glide them around the stage. The rainbow lamp clicks on. A highly passionate score kicks in as rainbow colours burst across the stage turning into a galaxy where mermaid projections swim. The boys twist and turn on the spot as if skiing before letting go. They slow-motion fall. The sound of a splash of water. All lighting returns to normal except the rainbow lamp.

DANIEL (*pulling himself up onto a trunk*). Woo. (*He lends a hand to* BOY.) There we go.

BOY (*out of breath*). I wanna do that forever.

The stage lighting flushes pink. Blackout.

A movement sequence occurs, going through the seasons of Halloween and Christmas, the cast all interacting with each other against a music score that shows the progression and development of BOY*'s friendships and his relationship with* DANIEL. *Though this should have a happy feel as a transition scene,* BOY*'s struggle begins to show.*

Scene Nine

Daniel's Monologue/Build a House

DANIEL *stands centre stage alone. As he talks, he packs the ski equipment back into the trunks and rearranges them into a bed.*

DANIEL. And that's how it started. Just like that. There was a lot to get my head around at first, little odd moments that somehow felt special. We couldn't have been more different. I was all race cars and nightclubs and he was all poetry and book clubs. But it worked. Whatever I needed him to be he merged into it, like a little chameleon. If I mentioned car engines by the next day he knew every part. He was a little piece of something entirely different and try as I might, I couldn't put my finger on why. Highly strung? Absolutely. A moral complex that would beat a saint up, but he was also everything I'd ever needed. Like a million little stars in one person. There was no topic out of bounds, no grounds undiscussed. I loved him. I mean I truly loved him… We spent days and nights planning forever like it was something you could touch. Something you pull into reality and hold close to you. Our entire lives planned out, where we'd live and what we'd do. How we'd build a home. As if you could use promises for nails and tile a roof in trust. Sat on a porch, grass a brilliant green, open a beer and just… be.

BOY enters, kisses DANIEL and sets himself down on one of the trunks.

BOY. Bedtime?

They both lie down on the trunks, the lights dim, DANIEL wraps his arm around BOY.

DANIEL. Goodnight.

IMAGINARY DANIEL enters. He is the same costume DANIEL wears and must embody his mannerism clearly. DANIEL remains in bed, BOY gets up.

BOY. Forever.

DANIEL and BOY's theme plays.

BOY yawns, clicks his fingers and the rainbow lamp ignites.

Through whatever means the set and stage allow, BOY must build a house for the two of them in which to live. He can use lighting and projection as well as physical set pieces. He stands back and admires his work before crawling back into bed.

Scene Ten

The Fire Eater

RACHEL *and* LARA *are on stage dissembling the house as if it were part of the circus set.*

LARA. Never thought they'd take off so quickly.

RACHEL. Yeah, well, me neither but at least they're happy.

> BOY *enters behind them, they don't notice him.*

LARA. Was it like this for you, Rach? When you were with him?

RACHEL. Yes and no, I think we socialised a little more.

LARA. I'm just a little worried.

RACHEL. Eh, whatever works for them.

LARA. Do you think he knows? I mean, about you two.

RACHEL. Nope. Wouldn't bet on it.

LARA. Why not?

RACHEL. I just wouldn't bet on it.

LARA. Is that a good thing? He seems sensitive.

RACHEL. He'll be fine. This isn't the army, it's not like climbing Everest, is it?

LARA. No, I guess not.

> *They exit.*

> BOY *sits on the remaining trunks left in the shape of a bed. His necklace pulses and the same loud electronic noises as previous are heard. He attempts to shake them off.*

> DANIEL *enters.*

DANIEL. Ripper of a training session, I've got the knees of an eighty-year-old at twenty-five. I swear to god if I have to do that circuit one more time I'm gonna explode.

BOY. When were you going to tell me about Rachel?

DANIEL. What?

BOY. You used to date Rachel?

DANIEL. We didn't date, we've been friends for ages.

BOY. Don't lie to me.

DANIEL. I'm not lying, babe.

BOY. Yes you are!

DANIEL. Babe, I have no reason to lie to you. We were not together.

BOY. So me overhearing the others today talking about it was just made up, was it?

Beat.

DANIEL. What?

BOY. When we got together you told me everyone you've been with, but you left out that one of our closest mates was one of them.

DANIEL. I didn't leave it out, it didn't happen.

They freeze.

EMILE *enters carrying a fire-eating torch and bottle of alcohol, he stands on the spot and, with a lighter, acts out igniting it. The stage lighting pulses from red to orange on him, imitating flames.*

BOY. So if I went and asked her she'd say no, would she? Would you be happy to come with me?

DANIEL. You're totally overreacting!

BOY (*increasingly passionate*). Am I? You told me, you told me you hadn't lied to me and now the girl I have to work with every single day, one of my friends. I feel like everyone's let in on a secret I'm not a part of.

EMILE *takes his first swig of alcohol, puts the torch to his lips and blows in the direction of the other two men.* BOY's *necklace pulses, the electronic noises increase and the sound of a dragon breathing fire is played. Both men react as if burned.*

DANIEL. Fucking hell, would you calm down. I'm sorry I wasn't as honest as you have been. I don't know why I didn't tell you, I'm sorry okay. It was nothing – nothing. It was a few months a long time back.

BOY. I don't understand why people lie, the truth is always there to see like a blood-splatter analysis at a crime scene. I love you, I just, I don't do well with surprises sometimes.

DANIEL. I messed up, I'll tell you the truth in future, I know you've always told me the truth about everything. I really am sorry.

Electronic noises pulse hard. BOY *is visibly struggling with the weight of the concealed necklace. He closes his eyes, strains, and all lighting turns to normal. The electronic buzz stops. He holds himself for a moment, visibly exceptionally uncomfortable and in pain.*

EMILE *swallows the lit torch.*

BOY *recoils in pain for a moment, staggers. Entirely unnoticed by* DANIEL. *The acting here must demonstrate the metaphorical swallowing and supressing of traits for the benefit of others to his own sacrifice.*

BOY. I love you.

DANIEL. I love you too.

Scene Eleven

The Failed Escape

BOY *and* DANIEL *take their places at the back of the stage for the original circus line-up. Spotlights roll around the stage and a crowd cheering is heard.* RACHEL, EMILE *and* LARA *join them in their positions.*

MALE VOICE-OVER. And now, ladies and gentlemen, our penultimate act for the evening, Our very own escape artist extraordinaire –

BOY *steps forward with* RACHEL *and* DANIEL *either side of him. From the trunk they both pull chains.*

He will now attempt to escape from his constraints in less than a hundred and twenty seconds on the clock.

RACHEL *and* DANIEL *begin to wrap and further padlock* BOY. *One chain for both his hands and one around his body, his necklace is on display.*

Thank you, Rachel. Thank you, Daniel, are we ready?

BOY *gives an unsure thumbs-up.*

And CLOCK.

A ticking timer is shown on the screen at the back of the stage.

RACHEL *and* DANIEL *step away.* BOY*'s necklace ignites. The same music as the audition sequence is heard but in a far more pained and uneasy way. Rainbow colours splash about the stage intermitted with electronic buzzing and strobe lighting.* BOY *is visibly struggling and in pain, trying to remove the chains. Throughout the music he fights with the chains as splashes of rainbow colours knock him back.* DANIEL *attempts to help but is knocked back by* BOY. *This sequence should be dramatic and uneasy to watch. As the timer ticks it becomes more and more evident he will not be successful in freeing himself this time. He manages to get the chains from his body off but falls to his knees as the timer* *buzzes out, his hands still tied. Boos and jeers are heard from the crowd as the lights flicker.*

Pause.

May I apologise on behalf of Kyō-Sō's circus for that technical issue. We do hope you enjoy the rest of your time here with us tonight. Moving swiftly on, our final act of the evening – our doubly-daring Dan in his strong-man act.

Circus music resumes, crowds begins to cheer once more, DANIEL *walks over to* BOY, *picks him up from his knees and carries him offstage. Circus music fades as cheers rain out.*

Scene Twelve

Boy and Daniel's Bedroom

DANIEL *sets an exhausted* BOY *down on the ground and proceeds to quickly assemble the bed from the trunks.*

BOY (*coming around*). I'm sorry.

DANIEL. Hey, don't be sorry.

BOY. No I *am* sorry.

DANIEL. You have nothing to apologise for. What happened out there?

BOY. I dunno I just, lost it for a second I think. I don't wanna talk about it.

DANIEL. I've seen that look on your face before. You know you can trust me, don't you?

BOY. I do, I just felt unwell. I've not been great recently.

DANIEL. Not to pry, babe, but that didn't look like you were just a little bit unwell. I've got you.

BOY. I do trust you.

DANIEL. That's not what I said, and you say that, but you're not that good an actor. At least not with me.

BOY. The Rachel conversation just fucked me up a little, that's all.

Beat.

DANIEL. I'm sorry.

BOY. Don't be. It's not your fault and we're over that now, sometimes things just get a little – (*Beat.*) heavy.

DANIEL. I'm here for you.

BOY. I know.

DANIEL. Always. Just explain what happened to them and they'll be fine. Just tell them you felt unwell. Tell them the truth.

BOY. That I felt unwell?

DANIEL. Yeah. That's the truth, isn't it?

BOY. Yes.

DANIEL. There. Now rest up. You're strong enough to handle this.

BOY. Not as strong as you.

DANIEL. You are.

BOY (*pause*). Daniel?

The music from the pond sequence with ABBY *plays.*

DANIEL. Yeah?

BOY. Never mind, it's nothing.

DANIEL. Okay, I'll come check on you again later

He kisses BOY*'s forehead. Sits on the edge of the bed and begins to sing 'Over the Rainbow'.* DANIEL *exits on 'Where you'll find me'.*

The lights dim as BOY *falls asleep, the screen at the back of the stage shows night to day.* BOY *gets up. Holds his necklace for a moment, sighs and begins to walk up stage. Circus lights spin and a complex soundtrack of music indicating confusion and disorientation plays.*

Scene Thirteen

A Circus Witch Trial

The cast arrange the trunks to resemble a courtroom. BOY *stands on one trunk centre stage. His hands bound by the* DOCTOR. WITNESS ONE *and* WITNESS TWO *assemble their trunks, they are open, facing them stage left forming the Jury Bench.* EMILE *enters wearing a judge's wig.* MOTHER *and* DOCTOR *sit either side of a trunk stage right. It must be clear that* MOTHER *and* DOCTOR *are not present in the court.*

DOCTOR. I believe what we may be dealing with here is Asperger's syndrome.

JUDGE. Today you stand accused of work malpractice, poor quality of performance and a poor attitude. How do you answer these charges?

BOY. Not guilty obviously.

MOTHER. Asperger's syndrome?

DOCTOR. Yes, nothing to worry about just expect low social development, panic attacks, the occasional outburst, confused concepts in all manner of life and very homed interests think of it like –

JUDGE. Last night you failed to perform your stunt to an adequate standard. Your dedication to your work and indeed to this circus is lacking considerably.

BOY. I –

JUDGE. Overruled. Call the first witness.

WITNESS ONE *gets up to stand aside* BOY.

MOTHER. Discourage abnormal behaviour? What? Tell him to suppress it? Is that what you're asking?

DOCTOR. Suppress is a big big word. You came with significant and valid concerns for your son's well-being and development. It's not too late for him, he's at a stage, as we've previously discussed, in which blending into the typical world is possible. To find the problems and stamp them out.

JUDGE. Witness One, present your evidence.

WITNESS ONE. The accused is rude, blunt and unwantedly honest. He actually tells people what he thinks. (*Beat.*) No I don't think you understand. He says what's on his mind out loud to the world. That isn't normal, is it? Saying what you think. In work. To your friends? People you trust? Unheard of. What happened to white lies? The most beautiful mechanism to gaslight those around you. Do I look good in this? (*Beat.*) Yesssss don't be silly you look lovely. I love the way you've matched chiffon with Crocs. It's a. Choice.

Instead he spends his time insulting those around him and bringing down the mood of the room. His lack of care for others' emotions is astounding. He clearly doesn't care about the feelings of people around him or indeed this show on the whole that he should be so grateful to be a part of.

BOY. That's not true I –

JUDGE. Overruled.

DOCTOR. For example, many people claim to prefer honest people over those who tell them what they want to hear but when it comes to fruition, they aren't so respondent. The inherent sincerity of an autistic individual can come over as exceptionally rude. This is just an example; there are, of course, other unacceptable societal behaviours.

MOTHER. And we can change that?

DOCTOR. With proper behaving therapies – yes .

JUDGE. Witness One, continue.

WITNESS ONE. The accused is shifty and a liar. It's all in the body language. This is obvious from his lack of engagement with others and reluctance to socialise. Try and make him give you eye contact. Liars can't make eye contact.

BOY. I –

JUDGE. Silence.

WITNESS ONE. Look at him now. He can barely look any of us in the eye.

JUDGE. Thank you, Witness One, come forward, Witness Two.

WITNESS ONE *takes her place and is replaced by* WITNESS TWO.

State your evidence.

WITNESS TWO. The accused is always off on some other planet barely concentrating on what it is he's meant to be doing. His attention to detail on pulling up others is extreme but exceptionally lax when it comes to himself and his own attitudes, often responding rudely and abruptly. His failure to carry out even the most simple of tasks is astonishing. Just yesterday I asked him 'Could you help me pack up please?' and do you know what his response was? 'Yes I can help you' and walked off. He actually walked off. Down the road. I'd asked for help.

BOY. Can and will are not the same thing.

WITNESS TWO. His rigid and inflexible attitude causes chaos amongst the cast. If it isn't done his way, it doesn't get done.

BOY. It's not like that.

WITNESS TWO. He seems to not be able to follow the simplest of instructions well at all. Like it's hard. Like it's climbing Everest equipped only with a Lucozade Sport and a –

BOY. That's –

JUDGE. Overruled.

MOTHER. What other challenges must we work on?

DOCTOR. Timing relies on working memory, multi-tasking and planning, all of which are typical executive functioning challenges some autistic people simply do not have the capacity for without rigorous help. Too many indirect demands can be confusing as can general social etiquette.

MOTHER. And if we give him rigorous enforcement, that'll work?

DOCTOR. Yes. That'll work. He'll always be autistic, but it'll be on the inside. Outwardly he'll appear entirely like everyone else.

MOTHER. And that'll be easy for him, will it?

DOCTOR. Well...

JUDGE. Thank you, Witness Two.

BOY. You're twisting the evidence.

JUDGE. Daniel was with him the night before last, before the incident. Do you have any reason to believe any external factors could have been at play to contribute to the accused failure to perform? This isn't the first time he's had issues. Communication, et cetera, seem to be a theme amongst cast mates.

DANIEL (*changing from* DOCTOR). He said he felt unwell.

WITNESS TWO. He's felt unwell a lot, hasn't he. The rest of us haven't.

JUDGE (*banging the gavel*). Order. Witnesses, take your seats.

MOTHER. He shouldn't have to suppress who he is.

DOCTOR. If he is allowed to carry out the world in his own way, a world of inward fantasy yet outward fear he will never progress into society normally.

MOTHER. But he'll be happier in himself?

DOCTOR. On the other hand, if we assist him into the world along a strict course he will be far more successful in all walks of life.

MOTHER. Isn't there another way?

BOY. This isn't a fair trial, this is a –

MOTHER. All of the doors will open for him this way but he may unintentionally close them as he trips over the traits he can't avoid. But if we don't, the doors will be closed from the off. I've seen the programmes. Read the forums. Know the stats. Seen the picket lines at the vaccine clinics. It's happening right now – out there. Tonight – (*She points to the back of the theatre. To the audience.*)

DOCTOR. Indeed. This is why I've advised it's best this topic be kept quiet from all teachers, friends and other parents, we don't wish the world to limit him now, do we? (*Beat.*) Do you know how disability is viewed?

MOTHER. This isn't fair this is a...

All freeze.

BOY. In 1612 many people faced trials for crimes they didn't commit based on the opinions of the locals in villages. Anyone who was different was set up and accused of witchcraft. The person would be bound and thrown into a river. If they sunk and drowned, they were innocent. If they floated, they were a witch and were hung. There was no winning either way.

All unfreeze.

JUDGE. Jury, make your verdict.

DOCTOR. A decision please?

The witnesses hold up 'Guilty' signs from their trunks.

MOTHER. But he can't change who he is? Surely? Could we be setting him up to fail?

DOCTOR. That's simply not possible. It'll work.

Beat.

BOY. Can we get a McDonald's on the way home?

MOTHER. Of course we can, darling.

Blackout.

Scene Fourteen

Head Above Water, Weight of the Worlds

MOTHER, DANIEL *and* LARA *are on stage.* BOY *stands central. His chains remain on his arms from the previous scene. A blue ripple spotlight is on him, illustrating water, the remainder of the cast walk around the set as memories of* BOY'*s childhood worlds are picked out of it. A flower from the jungle, etc.*

MOTHER. You carry a child for nine months and a new little world is created.

BOY. You grow up strong and humble yet bewildered and frustrated.

LARA. Surrounded by love of all those who know you.

DANIEL. Learning only how to love through the ways people show you.

MOTHER. But worlds can be heavy, weighted in a spin.

LARA. We all blend a little just trying to fit in.

DANIEL. Sacrifice who we are for the sake of each other.

MOTHER. Treasuring every moment just like I did his brother.

LARA. But there's a price you pay for every single bend you make.

DANIEL. The more you bend for others the sooner you will break.

LARA. I watched him for months keep his head above water.

MOTHER. Praying I didn't go and raise a pig for the slaughter.

DANIEL. The tides rose quickly and the tank started leaking.

LARA. Every day he played the part with less and less speaking.

MOTHER. I watched the weight fall off him with the world on on his back.

DANIEL. Carried him the best I could before I had to crack.

LARA. They argued more and more and whenever I lent a hand.

DANIEL. Pains me still I had to up and leave Neverland.

MOTHER. He'd call me every day when nobody was listening.

LARA. The rainbow lights behind his eyes began to stop glistening.

DANIEL. I'm strong enough for one world, enough of a man.

MOTHER. Wendy chose the London streets over Peter Pan.

LARA. The army man in him began to stand down.

DANIEL. I fought for air but one of us was surely gonna drown.

MOTHER. Stars burn out even those in our minds.

LARA. Wolves can only run so far before they're shot for hides.

DANIEL. Dragon fire destroys and burns cities to the fall.

MOTHER. Sirens catch sailors with their deathly call.

BOY. Days and nights merged in one as the worlds began to blend.

LARA. I tried to stand firm with him and be a decent friend.

DANIEL. It was like he wasn't him any more, he was off somewhere cold.

MOTHER. Lost at the rainbow's edge searching for the gold.

LARA. A boat can float on water as long as it is hollow.

BOY. Apologising nightly with the pride I had to swallow.

MOTHER. But add too much weight and your days get shorter.

DANIEL. I couldn't keep watching him keep his head above water.

BOY. But I stood and took it, firm on my feet standing.

MOTHER. Passengers, please prepare for an emergency landing.

MOTHER *and* LARA *exit.*

DANIEL *heads to where* BOY *is stood, pulls him from the water effect and all lights return to normal.*

BOY. This is it, isn't it? The end of forever.

DANIEL. Maybe.

BOY. Maybe isn't a thing.

DANIEL. I know.

BOY. Forever doesn't have an end.

DANIEL. This time it has to. For both our sakes. I can't carry this any more.

BOY. Figuratively?

DANIEL. Literally.

BOY (*holding in tears*). I love you.

DANIEL (*a tear falls down his cheek*). I love you too.

BOY. Please can we stay friends?

DANIEL. Always.

DANIEL *exits.*

BOY *falls to his knees.*

DOCTOR *and* MOTHER *enter.*

DOCTOR. It's not uncommon for autistic people to find one person they associate with more than anything, that bond clearly has already happened with yourself. But as he grows that bond will latch to other people – people who make him feel safe – loved, seen and supported. But that communication isn't considered normal. Too strong – too powerful – too uncensored.

MOTHER. I see, and how long does that last?

Beat.

BOY. What's at the end of forever?

MOTHER *and* DOCTOR *exit.*

Beat.

Running with wolves.

Build a house.

A castle in the skies.

Dragon rides?

His necklace will not glow. Nothing will glow. No illusions of fantasy, no music score. An empty, silent stage.

BOY *heaves himself across the stage and sits in the spot he stood moments ago. The water effect resumes. A timer begins to tick on screen, He begins to fight with the necklace without success. The crowd cheers. The lights dim slowly down. The sound of the house* BOY *and* DANIEL *built together crashing to ground is heard, The sound of crowds cheering reminiscent of Dorothy's arrival in Oz are heard.* BOY *reacts to nothing. House lights fade up. He composes himself, singing the first verse of 'Over the Rainbow' with no music or stage lighting. Lights down.*

(*To the necklace and composing himself.*) You think you're up for this? It's a lot to imagine and make real

Sound effect of Tinkerbell twinkle.

Let's see then. STOP.

The clock ticking stops.

Just. Change it all.

The clock resumes but this time backwards, picking up in speed. There should be audible ticking. The music speeding up in tempo giving the illusion of going backwards in time. The cast walk through the scene and interreact with each other at a super-fast pace. BOY *stops struggling. Each of them picks up a trunk and begins to move quickly, forming scenes that we've previously seen without stopping in them for more than a few seconds.*

The cast freeze with only DANIEL *left on stage with* IMAGINARY BOY. *The water effect resumes.* BOY *stands watching.*

FEMALE VOICE-OVER. This is a Midlands Rail Service to what should have happened.

DANIEL *puts his trunk down and sits upon it.*

DANIEL. Does a bear shit in the woods? Of course I'm certain, now are you coming or not?

BOY. No, thanks though, I'll sit this one out.

The water effect resumes and the timer keeps ticking. The scene clears as the cast continue to race around the stage. BOY *remains still.*

FEMALE VOICE-OVER. Arriving.

IMAGINARY BOY *stands alone centre stage.* BOY *watches.*

BOY. Thank you.

MALE VOICE-OVER. Will you work overseas?

BOY. Yes.

MALE VOICE-OVER. Will you commit to a year contract?

BOY. Yes.

MALE VOICE-OVER. Any medical conditions that might affect your work?

BOY. Autism. But it won't affect my work if there's changes, and you listen and we work together and we –

MALE VOICE-OVER. Thank you – but I don't think this opportunity is for you.

BOY. But I just showed you I can do it?

MALE VOICE-OVER. Thank you that'll be all.

The water effect resumes and the timer keeps ticking. The scene clears as the cast continue to race around the stage. BOY *remains still.*

FEMALE VOICE-OVER. Arriving.

ABBY *and* BOY *stand centre stage.*

BOY. So uh, what are you up to this weekend?

ABBY. Actually, me and a few friends are having a sleepover in a few days, would you like to come?

BOY. Oh, no thanks, I've got some things on.

The water effect resumes and the timer keeps ticking. The scene clears as the cast continue to race around the stage. BOY *remains still.*

FEMALE VOICE-OVER. Arriving.

MOTHER *and* DOCTOR *are on stage,* BOY *watches.*

MOTHER. You have to pray and pray you picked right.

DOCTOR. A decision please.

BOY. Don't do it, Mom – it isn't worth it.

MOTHER. I think he'll be fine just as he is actually. He has love. I'll give him the support he needs as will those around him. We'll all work at it.

The water effect resumes and the timer keeps ticking. The scene clears as the cast continue to race around the stage. BOY *remains still.*

FEMALE VOICE-OVER. Final Destination. All off.

The water effect spreads across the whole stage as the timer ends. BOY *steps forward into the scene. Sirens singing can be faintly heard. Two trunks are placed centre stage.*

BOY. Hello?

The stage echoes as if underwater, bubble effects rise.

MOTHER *enters.*

MOTHER. We wondered when we'd see you here again.

BOY. I can't be here, this has to go too.

MOTHER. Really? Pity. You used to love it here. You'd play here for hours – Come, sit, watch the sunrise with me.

BOY *and* MOTHER *take a seat on the trunks. In the distance sirens splashing and singing can be heard.*

You'd do that, would you? Change all of it? Yourself and all that you are?

BOY. Yes. To be normal. To fit in. To be accepted. Loved and for it to go right. To not swim upstream any more.

MOTHER. And what if you could have both? I'm just curious.

BOY. That's not possible. Curious of what?

MOTHER. To see what that man can do when the mask drops. To see the merging of worlds.

BOY. They're not compatible. That world isn't ready for this one.

MOTHER. Then make it be. There are other people like you too. You've just never met them.

The sun begins to rise.

I've often wondered. Who got the worse ending, Peter Pan or Wendy? We'll never really know but that's something I've thought about a lot.

BOY. Wendy.

MOTHER. You're sure?

BOY. Peter? Both.

MOTHER walks him to centre stage.

MOTHER. Then who got the better? They're just stories. But you – you're real, which makes this all real too. It isn't two worlds – it's one, and it always has been. And you belong in it.

She touches his head and a single spot appears on BOY. MOTHER shows she's holding a key, he reaches for it but immediately the clock begins to tick forwards. Rainbow lights pulse across the stage as the cast scurry around creating the illusion of time passing once more. The music begins to blur into that of the circus music. The water effect covering the whole stage slowly closes in to just the spotlight on BOY.

The timer tings.

BOY falls forward gasping for air as the circus crowd cheers.

Blackout.

Scene Fifteen

The Dream

Rainbow lights. BOY's necklace illuminates as he gets up out of bed. The howl of a wolf is heard. BOY and DANIEL's theme begins to play. DANIEL enters wearing a shirt and rainbow bow tie, MOTHER enters wearing a dress in rainbow print, THOMAS enters in a shirt and rainbow tie. EMILE enters wearing a shirt and rainbow circus top hat. DANIEL makes his way to BOY and they begin to slow dance as the remaining cast watch 'first dance' style. As the song plays out, the soundtrack blurs into the songs of mermaids, wolves howling and dragons flying. BOY and DANIEL kiss and continue to slow dance.

BOY. This isn't real, is it? This is another one of my…

DANIEL (*long beat*). No, this isn't real.

BOY. What am I supposed to do?

> DANIEL *positions* BOY *in front of him and pulls a key from his own pocket, presenting it forward.*

> (*Holding in tears.*) But this isn't real.

> *They resume slow dancing.*

DANIEL. You'll work it out.

> *The music slows as* BOY *looks over to the crowd of other cast stood stage left. As he does,* DANIEL *exits, as do the rest of the cast.* BOY *is left standing alone.*

> *The music stops.*

> BOY *stands for a moment before running to his bed, he grabs a trunk, throws the mermaid blanket inside and runs offstage. The sound of an airplane taking off.*

Scene Sixteen

The Final Flight

The entire cast enter and assume their seats on the plane.

MOTHER/HOSTESS. Welcome on board this 1401 service – home. The date is March 23rd 2020, the sky is blue, the wind is up – out of your passenger windows you can see it's about to start raining

BOY. Cats and dogs.

> *All members of the ensemble take an oxygen mask from below their chairs and place it over their nose and mouth. They move in slow motion. All but* BOY *seem panicked.*

(*Sitting on the edge of the stage*.) It wasn't easy, was it? Not quite what we'd all thought? Come on, everyone, just be normal. Just adapt, just fucking get on with it. Change, what's the matter with all of you? Struggling? I get it – masking up can feel a little tight around the edges. A little locked in. A little closed off. A little separated from the world. I suppose you could spend the next two years making your own worlds to live in, couldn't you? Learn to understand people through the panic. It's not that hard surely. I'm not gonna judge you for it, am I? But wow would you stop taking the news so fucking literally. That's not what's happening at all. Life can't always be black and white, you know. Raining cats and dogs now. Maybe maybe maybe, isn't it great. I love it. We all know I love it. Don't you all want more of that? Well, we've got another six months in store for all of you at least. It's only the uncertain, what like it's hard?

Beat.

I'm autistic. There. You all now know, don't you. I fucking said it. Maybe now you get it. You get what it feels like. It's ugly, it's uncomfortable, it's confusing, it's horrific, living in a world you don't understand and that doesn't understand you. I've been on Zoom calls my entire life. I've been reading above the face mask since day dot. I've been socially distanced from birth. I've been learning new certainties and had them ripped away from me for so long... But it is also the most beautiful world I have ever known. My brain is a concept that defeats itself – it isn't binary. No matter how hard it wants to be.

I'm autistic and that's not always pretty. That's not always easy. But what it can be is fascinating, beautiful, kind, loving, different, unique. You just have to give us the chance. It can be like swimming in an ocean of diamonds and jumping over the moon with just your bare two feet. It can be like riding through a galaxy all alone but entirely surrounded by all you ever needed. I just need you all to see it.

I love you all so much, SO much I can barely contain it.

I can barely breathe and if you walk away now you walk away. But I couldn't hide it any more. I'm not a bad person. I'm not a hateful person. But I can't keep blending for your sake. I'm sorry. This world can take me as I am or not at all. I've lost too much your way, I've given too much but it wasn't enough. We've gotta try my way. We can't keep sacrificing who we are to please others. None of us.

BOY *puts his hand into his own pocket. Pulls out a key, sticks it into the lock and removes the chain. From the plane we merge into everyday life on stage. The same music as the 'wolves' sequence plays in a far slower and violin-heavy melody... The music is a peaceful and beautiful symphony. He stands tall and drops the necklace to the floor. The bang should be so loud as it hits that people would imagine he just dropped a massive weight. The screen at the back of the stage shows mermaids swimming, The wolves run wild, the planets come back to life.* BOY *stands defiant and tall. For the first time all of the other cast are able to see the illusions too, each one of them interreacting with a different one. The two worlds blend. Each of the characters take their turns in embracing him. His* MOTHER *last. She holds him and kisses his forehead. All of the cast leave bar* MOTHER, *the ocean waves crash, the stage turns to that of a beach and they sit together.*

MOTHER. Tomorrow's going to be better.

BOY. Do you promise?

He leans his head on her shoulder, fade to black, one final splash is heard.

The silhouette of a small dragonfly flies across the screen, sits for a moment then takes off.

Testimonials

JJ Green (*playwright, actor*)

Having this play published, produced and put on is something I never thought could happen. My reasoning behind that thinking is that until I was twenty-five nobody even knew I was autistic. I thought it was a dirty, dark little secret and I held it in from the rest of the world close to my chest for all those years, and had a series of unfortunate events not taken place – I probably still would be holding onto it today. I hid who I was, to my own massive detriment both mentally and physically, for fear of how the truth would affect me. I did this because that fear was not irrational. This world is not a kind place to people like me and we are led to believe that if we can disguise, we can survive.

Sharing this story with the world is a huge step but nothing compared to sharing the truth about my autism with that very first person. Over the last few years, step by step and inch by inch led me here. The unpicking that comes with deciding you're valid for exactly who you are despite always believing otherwise is long and arduous. Learning to love yourself when you've been led to believe who you are is faulty is complex. Complex but possible.

I am eternally grateful that the place in which this play was born is no longer a place I inhabit, but I am aware that for many many others – they still live there. I hope this play provides solace, solidarity, empathy and understanding to autistic people who've felt othered by the world in which we live. I hope it makes them laugh. I hope it elevates their voices and their courage and I hope that in some small way it can make autistic people feel less alone. Even if it's just the one. That'll be enough.

My eternal thanks go out to Katy Lipson of Aria Entertainments for producing this play. To Bronagh Lagan and the creative team for bringing it to life and finally to the people who've loved me as I unpicked exactly who I am these last few years. This feeling really is golden.

Tomorrow will be a better one. I promise.

Conor Joseph (*actor*)

Among other things *A-Typical Rainbow* is a wonderfully generous script. JJ's writing invites artists from across disciplines to come together, collaborate on, and be a part of telling this story. That so many of the artists that make up the cast and creatives share experiences with the character's feels precious, and to work as part of a creative team so close to the script has been an enormous privilege. With personal connection comes depth of feeling, an appreciation of nuance, and an understanding that experiences don't just end when the lights go up. *A-Typical Rainbow* ends with a question, and I'm delighted to be a part of asking it.

Caroline Deverill (*actor*)

When I saw the announcement that Aria Entertainment were producing a new play which is an authentic account of growing up autistic and queer, it made me incredibly emotional. I am a mum, and my beautiful son, Cooper, is autistic. Every time I see someone working to increase acceptance and throw a spotlight on the changes needed to make society more inclusive, it gives me hope for his future, negotiating this world.

The fact that I then got an audition for this incredible play, and won the role of Mother, was unbelievable! The stars aligned.

I feel immensely proud and privileged to be a part of this company and to share this amazing piece with everyone.

Thank you Aria Entertainment for seeing how important a project this is, and especially thank you JJ for writing such a beautiful and vital play.

Joy Tan (*actor*)

You can't surgically remove your neurodivergence to experience life without it – people often ask me 'How has ADHD changed your life?' I have no idea, because it *is* my life. It's not wrong or bad: ADHD simply manifests in aspects of me that are more saturated than most.

Think of this: you cannot tell me with 100% certainty that everyone experiences the exact same blue, and yet nobody assumes otherwise. To me, *A-Typical Rainbow* shares *blue* with those watching, introducing it to your colour scheme, yet without prescribing it as the only true way of seeing.

Right now, stories shared from personal experience are vitally important. It's not impossible to write a nuanced story without it – but there's true poignancy in writing what you know, and nothing more beautiful than finally seeing yourself truly reflected in it.

Here's hoping experiencing this play helps you share your blue sky with others, or maybe helps you feel the shape of their horizon.

Maya Manuel (*actor*)

To me, *A-Typical Rainbow* is such a touching play on the experience of neurodivergence. I too have members of my family that are neurodivergent and thus see the world in a different way. It's easy to fear the way others view the world, especially if it contrasts so much with how you think you view the world. But in many ways this is a beautiful, unique experience, that I don't think we should fear, but embrace and adapt our world around. Not changing the people to fit in the world, but transforming our world so everyone feels like they fit in.

James Westphal (*actor*)

I feel really privileged to have had the chance to be involved
with JJ's brilliant and vital new play. Being someone who lives
with OCD and ADD, having the chance to work in a room with
other neurodiverse creatives and creatives that have close
experiences with neurologically atypical disorders has been a
really special and rare experience that has meant a lot to me.
I haven't ever seen a piece of theatre that centers around an
autistic character written by an autistic writer, so this has felt
extremely authentic and delicately handled by all involved and
it's been a special experience to help bring to life a play that,
whilst showing the realities and struggles that neurodiverse and
specifically autistic people can face whilst trying to navigate a
world constructed mostly by and for neurotypical people, looks
to celebrate everyone's uniqueness. I've been on a big journey
over the last few years of learning to accept the ways in which
my brain works, and this play and process has been a brilliant
reminder that we must celebrate our uniqueness and
individuality as humans and harness it. There has been a real
sense of understanding, empathy and celebration within the
rehearsal room and it's an experience I know I'll treasure.
Thank you to everyone involved for this opportunity.

Ryan Webster (*deputy stage manager*)

It is an honour to be a small part of the staging of A-*Typical
Rainbow*, a first of its kind, a celebration of neurodivergency
and queerness. An incredibly touching, gritty and colourful
story through imagery and text that really leaves a resonant
mark. I'd like to thank JJ, Aria and Bronagh for allowing this
integral and truly reflective story to be told on behalf of our
communities in such vibrance and nuance that I think truly
reflects us as neurodivergent, queer people in a true captivating
light. This is representation at its finest – Representation
matters.

William Spencer (*choreographer*)

I am so humbled to be working as a choreographer on the first production of this play. It's amazing to me that something so full of fantasy can bring the realities of an autistic life to the stage. Having trained in classical ballet since the age of three, the rigorous routine and structure allowed me to navigate my struggles with motor skills and coordination, challenges which are faced by many neurodiverse people. This is why I'm particularly delighted to be showing another facet of what neurodiverse people can do. My favourite line in the play reads 'This world, seeing who we are – is rare.' This marks the first time, not only seeing someone like myself authentically represented on stage, but being in the room with those from my community during its creation. As the work I make is largely driven and informed by my neurodiversity, this production realises my own childhood fantasies of bringing stories to life. Because of the inclusion, diversity and acceptance of the team this experience has been truly affirming. Lastly, I would like to thank Katy, JJ and Bronagh for their support, strength and trust.

Max Alexander-Taylor (*composer and sound designer*)

When JJ approached me about composing for his show, I felt a real sense of opportunity like no other. We could do anything. We could let our imaginations flood the stage and be as bold as we wanted. I found out I was autistic at the age of fourteen. It was a diagnosis that helped me clarify some of the confusions I'd felt throughout my life, but also delivered some fresh challenges. This project has been an exercise in rediscovering and exploring those challenges and clarifications in my life – and along the way I've had fresh realisations; realisations that should help us to create imaginative and bold music and theatre. Hopefully by discovering something new about ourselves during this process, an audience will discover something new about themselves, too.